Lecture Notes in Computer Science   9325

Commenced Publication in 1973
Founding and Former Series Editors:
Gerhard Goos, Juris Hartmanis, and Jan van Leeuwen

More information about this series at http://www.springer.com/series/7408

Alberto Pardo · S. Doaitse Swierstra (Eds.)

Programming Languages

19th Brazilian Symposium SBLP 2015
Belo Horizonte, Brazil, September 24–25, 2015
Proceedings

 Springer

Editors
Alberto Pardo
Universidad de la República
Montevideo
Uruguay

S. Doaitse Swierstra
Utrecht University
Utrecht
The Netherlands

ISSN 0302-9743   ISSN 1611-3349   (electronic)
Lecture Notes in Computer Science
ISBN 978-3-319-24011-4   ISBN 978-3-319-24012-1   (eBook)
DOI 10.1007/978-3-319-24012-1

Library of Congress Control Number: 2015949737

LNCS Sublibrary: SL3 Programming and Software Engineering

Springer Cham Heidelberg New York Dordrecht London

Printed on acid-free paper

Springer International Publishing AG Switzerland is part of Springer Science+Business Media
(www.springer.com)

Preface

This volume contains the proceedings of the 19th Brazilian Symposium on Programing Languages (SBLP 2015), held during September 24–25, 2015, in Belo Horizonte, Brazil. SBLP is a well-established symposium, promoted by the Brazilian Computer Society since 1996, which provides a venue for researchers and practitioners interested in the fundamental principles and innovations in the design and implementation of programming languages and systems. Since 2010, SBLP has been organized in the context of CBSoft (Brazilian Conference on Software: Theory and Practice), co-located with a number of other events on computer science and software engineering.

The Program Committee of SBLP 2015 was formed by 33 members from 8 countries. The symposium received 26 submissions, including 4 short papers, with authors from four different countries. Each paper was reviewed by at least three reviewers, and evaluated on quality, originality, and relevance to the symposium. The final selection was made by the program co-chairs, based on the reviews and Program Committee discussion. The final program featured two keynote talks by Armando Fox (University of California at Berkerley) and Doaitse Swierstra (Utrecht University), one tutorial, nine full papers in English, a short paper in English, and two papers in Portuguese (presented at the conference, but not included in these proceedings).

We would like to thank the authors, the reviewers, and the members of the Program Committee for contributing to the success of SBLP 2015. We thank Armando Fox for accepting our invitation and enriching the technical program with an interesting talk. We also want to thank the members of the Organizing Committee of CBSoft 2015 for all their help and support. We do not want to conclude without expressing our gratitude to Fernando Pereira, chair of the SBLP Steering Committee and member of the organization of CBSoft 2015, for all his support at the different stages of the organization of the symposium.

July 2015

Alberto Pardo
S. Doaitse Swierstra

Organization

Organizing Committee

Eduardo Figueiredo	UFMG, Brazil
Fernando Pereira	UFMG, Brazil
Kecia Ferreira	CEFET-MG, Brazil
Maria Augusta Nelson	PUC-MG, Brazil

Program Committee Chairs

Alberto Pardo	Universidad de la República, Uruguay
Doaitse Swierstra	Utrecht University, The Netherlands

Program Committee

Alberto Pardo	Universidad de la República, Uruguay
Alex Garcia	IME, Brazil
Alvaro Moreira	Federal Univeristy of Rio Grande do Sul, Brazil
André Rauber Du Bois	Federal University of Pelotas, Brazil
Carlos Camarão	Federal University of Minas Gerais, Brazil
Christiano Braga	Fluminense Federal University, Brazil
Doaitse Swierstra	Utrecht University, The Netherlands
Fabio Mascarenhas	Federal University of Rio de Janeiro, Brazil
Fernando Pereira	Federal University of Minas Gerais, Brazil
Fernando Castor	Federal University of Pernambuco, Brazil
Francisco H. de Carvalho Junior	Federal University of Ceará, Brazil
Hans-Wolfgang Loidl	Heriot-Watt University, UK
João Saraiva	University of Minho, Portugal
João Ferreira	Teesside University, UK
Louis-Noel Pouchet	University of California Los Angeles/Ohio State University, USA
Lucília Figueiredo	Federal University of Ouro Preto, Brazil
Luís Barbosa	University of Minho, Portugal
Manuel A. Martins	University of Aveiro, Portugal
Marcelo A. Maia	Federal University of Uberlândia, Brazil
Marcelo d'Amorim	Federal University of Pernambuco, Brazil
Mariza Bigonha	Federal University of Minas Gerais, Brazil
Martin Musicante	Federal Univeristy of Rio Grande do Norte, Brazil
Noemi Rodriguez	PUC-Rio, Brazil
Peter Mosses	Swansea University, UK

Rafael Lins	Federal University of Pernambuco, Brazil
Roberto Bigonha	Federal University of Minas Gerais, Brazil
Roberto Ierusalimschy	PUC-Rio, Brazil
Rodrigo Ribeiro	Federal University of Ouro Preto, Brazil
Sandro Rigo	State University of Campinas, Brazil
Sérgio Medeiros	Federal University of Rio Grande do Norte, Brazil
Simon Thompson	University of Kent, UK
Varmo Vene	University of Tartu, Estonia
Zongyan Qiu	Peking University, China

Additional Reviewers

Apinis, Kalmer
Garcia, Maxiwell
Luna, Carlos
Mendes, Alexandra
Moreira, João

Nestra, Härmel
Pinto, Gustavo
Soares-Neto, Francisco
Vojdani, Vesal

Contents

Automatic Inference of Loop Complexity Through Polynomial Interpolation

Francisco Demontiê, Junio Cezar, Mariza Bigonha,
Frederico Campos, and Fernando Magno Quintão Pereira[✉]

UFMG, Avenida Antônio Carlos, 6627, Belo Horizonte 31270-010, Brazil
{demontie,juniocezar,mariza,ffcampos,fernando}@dcc.ufmg.br

Abstract. Complexity analysis is an important activity for software engineers. Such an analysis can be specially useful in the identification of performance bugs. Although the research community has made significant progress in this field, existing techniques still show limitations. Purely static methods may be imprecise due to their inability to capture the dynamic behaviour of programs. On the other hand, dynamic approaches usually need user intervention and/or are not effective to relate complexity bounds with the symbols in the program code. In this paper, we present a hybrid technique that solves these shortcomings. Our technique uses a numeric method based on polynomial interpolation to precisely determine a complexity function for loops. Statically, we determine: (i) the inputs of a loop, i.e., the variables that control its iterations; and (ii) an algebraic equation relating the loops within a function. We then instrument the program to plot a curve relating inputs and number of operations executed. By running the program over different inputs, we generate sufficient points for our interpolator. In the end, the complexity function for each loop is combined using an algebra of our own craft. We have implemented our technique in the LLVM compiler, being able to analyse 99.7 % of all loops available in the Polybench benchmark suite, and most of the loops in Rodinia. These results indicate that our technique is an effective and useful way to find the complexity of loops in high-performance applications.

1 Introduction

Complexity analyses show how algorithms scale as a function of their inputs. Its importance stems from the fact that such a technique helps program developers to uncover performance bugs which are hard to find. In addition to this, complexity analysis supports the decision of offloading or not computation to the cloud or GPU. Finally, this kind of technique has implications to the theoretical computer science community, as it provides data that corroborate the formal asymptotic analysis of algorithms. Given this importance, it comes as no surprise that, since the 70s [20], large amounts of effort have been spent in the design and improvement of empirical methodologies to infer code complexity.

Over the time, different static approaches were proposed to analyze programs in functional [6,15,20] and imperative [11–13] languages. Although the static

© Springer International Publishing Switzerland 2015
A. Pardo and S.D. Swierstra (Eds.): SBLP 2015, LNCS 9325, pp. 1–15, 2015.
DOI: 10.1007/978-3-319-24012-1_1

approaches have the benefit of running fast and may give correct upper bounds, this methodology has shortcomings. Static analyses may yield imprecise – or even incorrect – results. This imprecision happens due to the inherently inability of purely static approaches to capture the dynamic behavior of programs. In order to circumvent this limitation of static approaches, the programming language community has resorted to profiling-based methodologies [4,9,22]. However, even these dynamic techniques are not free of limitations.

The main drawback of a profiling-based complexity analysis is the fact that it is usually ineffective to relate the symbols in the program text to the result that it delivers. For instance, the state-of-the-art tool in this field is `aprof` [4]. Aprof furnishes programmers with a table that relates input sizes with the number of operations performed. This modus operandi has two problems, in our opinion. First, the input is provided as a number of memory cells read during the execution of a function. This number may not be meaningful to the programmer, as we will clarify in Sect. 2. Second, it works at the granularity of functions. However, developers are often more interested in knowing the computational complexity of small regions within a function. Such regions can be, for instance, performance-intensive loops. This paper addresses these two limitations of input sensitive profiling.

The main contribution of our work is a novel hybrid technique to perform complexity analysis on imperative programs, which we describe in Sect. 3. Our technique is hybrid because it combines static analysis with dynamic profiling. First, we use static analysis to determine loop inputs and to find algebraic relations between these loops. Then, we use a dynamic profiler, plus polynomial interpolation, to infer the complexity of each loop in a function. Our technique is capable of generating symbolic expressions that denote the complexity of each loop, instead of the whole function. Furthermore, we combine and simplify these expressions to make them even more meaningful to the software engineer. We believe that this granularity can help developers to have a deeper understanding of a function's behaviour; hence, it provides them with the means to detect and solve performance bugs more efficiently. We also show that our technique is simpler than previous work while producing more useful results.

We have designed, tested, and implemented a tool on top of the LLVM compilation infrastructure [14] to infer, automatically, the complexity of loops within programs. We ran our tool over the Polybench [19] and Rodinia [3] benchmark suites. Section 4 reports our findings. Our results indicate that we are capable of correctly inferring the complexity of 99.7 % of the Polybench loops and 69.18 % of the Rodinia loops. All the equations that we output, as explained in detail in Sect. 2, are written as functions of the symbols, i.e., variable names, present in the program code – that is an improvement on top of `aprof` and similar tools. Moreover, we have found that 38 % of all functions in the benchmarks that we analyzed have at least two independent loops. In this case, tools that only report complexity information for entire functions may miss important details about the asymptotic behaviour of smaller regions of code.

```
1:  void multiply(int **matA, int **matB, int n){
2:      int i, j, k, sum;
3:      int **result = (int**) malloc(n * sizeof(int*));
4:      for (i = 0; i < n; i++)
5:          result[i] = (int*) malloc(n * sizeof(int));
6:
7:      for (i=0; i < n; i++) {
8:        for (j=0; j < n; j++) {
9:          sum = 0;
10:          for (k=0; k < n; k++) {
11:            sum += matA[i][k] * matB[k][j];
12:          }
13:          result[i][j] = sum;
14:        }
15:      }
16:
17:      j = 0;
18:      for (i = 0; i < n;) {
19:        if (j >= n) {
20:          j = 0;
21:          i++;
22:          printf("\n");
23:        } else {
24:          printf("%8d", result[i][j++]);
25:        }
26:      }
27:      printf("\n");
28: }
```

Fig. 1. Matrix multiplication – the running example that we shall use to explain our contributions.

2   Overview

In this section we give an overview of the challenges this paper addresses. Figure 1 shows the example we will use to illustrate our technique. Function *multiply* is a routine that performs matrix multiplication of two square matrices. For pedagogical purposes, our function does not return the resulting matrix; instead, it prints the result. We chose to implement the function in such a way to show how our technique behaves on functions with multiple loops.

As developers, we would like to know the computational cost to execute this function. For instance, knowing the complexity of each part of the target function, we can find out performance bottlenecks and improve its implementation. Looking at the *multiply* function we can easily identify the linear behavior of the loop on line 4 and the cubic behavior of the nested loops beginning at line 7. However, a quick visual inspection on the loop at line 18 may not capture its quadratic complexity (Fig. 1).

```
index % time    self  children   name
[1]    100.0    0.00    0.03     main [1]
                0.03    0.00     multiply(int**, int**, int) [2]
                0.00    0.00     initArray(int**, int, int) [9]
                0.00    0.00     free_all(int**, int**, int) [10]
-----------------------------------------------------
                0.03    0.00     main [1]
[2]    100.0    0.03    0.00     multiply(int**, int**, int) [2]
-----------------------------------------------------
```

Fig. 2. Gprof output for a simple program containing our example function.

Input size	Average Cost
138	1111
174	3324
286	12007
367	18576
463	26694
575	36394
701	47749
846	60781
1007	75587

Fig. 3. The output produced by the aprof input sensitive profiler.

We can use profilers to find out where the program is spending most of its resources. However, traditional tools lack the ability to show how the program scales as a function of its inputs. For instance, Fig. 2 shows the output that Gprof [10] – the most well-known profiler in the Unix systems – produces for our example. This profiler does not give us any information regarding the asymptotic complexity of the program in Fig. 1. Instead, it produces a table describing where the program spends more time during its execution.

There exist profilers that have been designed specifically to provide developers with an idea about the asymptotic complexity of programs [4,9,22]. Nevertheless, aprof [4], the state-of-the-art approach in this field, is also not very useful in this example. For instance, only looking at Fig. 2, which shows aprof's results for the function *multiply*, the user may not fully understand about the function behaviour: this table shows numbers, but do not relate these numbers with symbols in the program text. Moreover, the complexity curve seems to be linear, since aprof considers the whole matrices as inputs (n^2) – usually, developers describe asymptotic complexity in terms of the matrices dimensions (n). Finally, the result generated by aprof describes the whole function. We believe that this granularity is too coarse, because it makes it very difficult for the user to verify the behavior of particular parts of the function.

We can do better: the technique that we describe in this paper produces one polynomial for each loop in the function. These polynomials range on symbols defined in the program text, e.g., the names of variables. Therefore, we claim that our output is clearer to the developer. For instance, considering the loop in line 7, we will state – automatically – that its complexity polynomial is: $n + 1$. Furthermore, considering the loop nest starting in line 18, we produce the following equation to denote its complexity polynomial: $n^2 + n + 1$.

Our result is on a finer granularity, so we can combine them to generate an equation that expresses the asymptotic behavior of the whole target function. For the function in the Fig. 1, our approach generates the following simplified equation, in big O, to denote the function's complexity:

$$O(n^3)$$

We claim that this notation, which uses the names of variables present in the program, is more meaningful to the application developer than the output produced by traditional profilers, such as *gprof* or `aprof`.

3   Complexity Analysis

We can describe our technique in four main steps: (1) static analysis, (2) code instrumentation, (3) dynamic information extraction and (4) polynomial interpolation. In this section we describe each one of these steps. However, before delving into the details of our technique, we shall introduce some notation, which will guide our explanations henceforth.

Loop Jargon. Let S be a subset of nodes of a control flow graph G. S contains a special node H, which we shall call *header*, or *entry point*. Following Appel and Palsberg [2, p. 376], we say that S is a *natural loop* if, and only if, it presents the following three properties:

1. there exists a path from any node in S to H;
2. there exists a path from H to any node in S;
3. there is no path from a node of G to a node of S that does not go across H.

The last property defines S as a *single-entry* region, following Ferrante's nomenclature [8]. An edge between any node in S to H is called a *back-edge*. We adopt Wolfe's definition of *trip count* [21, p. 200]: the number of times any back-edge of a natural loop has been traversed by the program flow within a single execution of the loop. Hence, a loop that exits the first time it is executed has a trip count of zero. The number of times H is visited is one more than the trip count of the loop. We estimate the *complexity* of a loop as the product of its trip count by the number of operations in its longest path.

We call a node $L \in S$ a *latch*, or *exit point*, if there exists an edge from L to a node N, $N \in G$, $N \notin S$. We say that L is a *natural latch* if one of these two conditions applies:

- $L = H$. In this case we have a *while loop*;
- $L \neq H$, and any edge from L either leaves S or leads to H. In this case we have a *repeat loop*.

If S contains only one latch, then we call it *single exit*. In this work we consider multiple exit loops featuring only one natural latch. Code generated from typical programming language constructs, i.e., `for`, `while` and `repeat` has this property, as long as the command `goto` is not used.

Any latch contains a *stop condition*: a boolean expression whose evaluation either keeps the program flow in S or leads away from it. If the natural latch contains a stop condition that uses only one operator, which can be either $<$, $\leq$, $>$ or $\geq$, then we call S an *interval loop*. We let the operands of the stop condition be the *limits* of the interval. For instance, in the interval loop `for(i = 0; i < N; i++)`, we have the stop condition `i < N`, whose limits are `i` and `N`. Our technique handles any loop with only one input, and interval loops with up to two inputs i_1 and i_2. In this case, we consider as the input size the difference $|i_1 - i_2|$.

3.1 Input Analysis

We start the process of inferring the complexity of code with a static analysis phase. The static analysis determines the inputs of each loop in the function. We qualify as *loop input* any data that:

– influences the stop condition of the loop; and,
– is not defined within the loop.

For instance, the loop at line 7 in Fig. 1 is controlled by $i < n$. Variable i has two definitions: one outside the loop, which we shall call i_0, and another inside, which we shall call i_1. The former is initialized with the constant zero, which is thus considered a loop input. Variable n is a parameter of the function; hence, it is considered a symbolic input. Therefore, the two inputs of the loop that exists at line 7 are $\{0, n\}$. Concretely, we detect inputs through a *backward* analysis, that starts at the variables used in the loop's stop condition, and ends at the definitions of variables that lay outside the loop body. To determine the complexity of a loop, we will plot the number of operations executed by the loop for each value bound to one of its inputs that we have observed during a profiling step. We shall describe this profiling in Sect. 3.3

3.2 Loop Dependence Analysis

Our profiler outputs the complexity of all the loops within a program. We must combine this information to have a snapshot of the program's complexity. However, combining the complexity of all the loops that constitute a program is not a straightforward problem. One of the main difficulties that we face in this case is how to deal with loops that may, or may not, execute, depending on the path that the program follows. In order to provide meaningful answers to the user, we propose an algebra to simplify the equations that we produce. Our algebra has three operators: *plus* ($+$), *times* ($\times$) and *expander* ($\oplus$). The *plus* and *times* operators have the usual semantics of asymptotic analysis. The expander was

```
1:  void printDups(std::vector<std::string> lines , std::string key) {
2:    std::vector<std::string> result;
3:    for (int i=0; i < lines.size(); i++) {
4:      if (lines[i].find(key) != std::string::npos) {
5:        result.push_back(lines[i]);
6:      }
7:    }
8:
9:    if (result.empty()) return;
10:
11:   // find dups in a naive way
12:   for (int i=0; i < result.size()-1; i++) {
13:     for (int j=i+1; j < result.size(); j++) {
14:       if (i != j && result[i] == result[j])
15:         std::cout << result[i] << std::endl;
16:     }
17:   }
18: }
```

Fig. 4. A function to print duplicate lines containing a given key. The second loop has a conditional execution.

proposed by us as an alternative to describe the complexity of code that may or may not execute, depending on the program's flow. Its semantics is defined in the Eqs. 1 and 2:

$$O(x^a \oplus y^b) = O(x^a) + O(x^b), \quad \{a,b\} \in \mathbb{N} \tag{1}$$

$$\Omega(x^a \oplus y^b) = \Omega(x^a), \quad \{a,b\} \in \mathbb{N} \tag{2}$$

As a reminder, the big-Omega notation indicates a lower asymptotic bound: $\Omega(f)$ denotes a function whose growth is less than or equal to the growth of f. Expansion denotes the complexity of code that executes conditionally. Figure 4 provides an example of a situation where the expander operation is useful. The function *printDups* prints the duplicate lines containing a given substring in a naive way. Because of the conditional branch in line 9, the loop starting on line 12 may or may not execute. Because of this, the complexity of this function is $\Omega(n)$ - best case, when no line contains the key - and $O(n^2)$, where n is the size of the vector. If $C(L)$ denotes the asymptotic complexity of a given code region, then we let $C(printDups) = C(L_{3-7}) \oplus C(L_{12-17}) = O(n \oplus n^2)$, where L_{3-7} is the loop at lines 3 to 7 in Fig. 4, and L_{12-17} is the loop at lines 12 to 17.

As usual, addition and multiplication in the big-O notation are associative and commutative. Multiplication is also distributive with regard to addition. On the other hand, *expansion* is only associative, due to Eq. 2. These properties let us use typical simplification rules to provide users of our tool with more palatable results. Notice, once again, that expansion is non-commutative, and simplification only applies if the first operand has higher complexity than the second:

$$\frac{C(L) = O(x^a) + O(x^b), a \geq b}{C(L) = O(x^a)}$$

$$\frac{C(L) = O(x^a) \times O(x^b)}{C(L) = O(x^{a+b})}$$

$$\frac{C(L) = O(x^a) + O(x^b), a < b}{C(L) = O(x^b)}$$

$$\frac{C(L) = O(x^a) \oplus O(x^b), a \geq b}{C(L) = O(x^a)}$$

The simplification process is guaranteed to terminate, as it always reduces the size of the resulting expression. Looking back to Fig. 1 it is easy to see that the complexity is $C(multiply) = C(L_{4-5}) + C(L_{7-15}) \times C(L_{8-14}) \times C(L_{10-12}) + C(L_{18-26})$, which gives us: $O(n + n * n * n + n^2)$. Using the above equations we can recursively simplify this expression. Firstly, we can simplify $n * n$ with n^2. We have now $O(n + n^2 * n + n^2)$ and we can use the same rule to simplify the remaining multiplication, resulting in n^3. It is easy to see that we can use the two rules of *plus* to simplify the two additions. Then, the resulting complexity is $O(n^3)$, as expected. Notice that n is a symbol produced by the input analysis of Sect. 3.1.

3.3   Code Instrumentation

We infer the complexity of code by analyzing profiling data. We produce this data through code instrumentation. To be able to extract dynamic information, we instrument the target program to output: (i) the values of the loop inputs immediately before the loop execution and (ii) the number of operations performed by each loop. Loop inputs are determined by the analysis seen in Sect. 3.1. The execution cost is measured in terms of instructions executed. We have implemented this instrumentation framework within the LLVM compiler infrastructure.

Care must be taken with regard to loops with multiple paths. Different paths may yield different costs, a fact that could hinder our interpolator from finding a perfect polynomial fit. Figure 5 illustrates this shortcoming. The program seen in part (a) of the figure contains two loops, at lines 2 and 4. The loop at line 4 contains two execution paths. Let's assume that during execution, our profiler has observed that for $M = 1$, that loop executed 44 instructions, and for $M = 2$, it always took the cheapest path; hence, executing $3+3$ operations. These points, $(1, 42), (2, 6)$ would confuse our interpolator, which expects more operations for larger inputs. To avoid this problem, we consider that the cost of a loop is determined by its path of highest cost, which we estimate statically. To obtain a conservative estimate of this path, we resort to a modified version of Dijkstra's algorithm, to solve the single-source largest path problem for an acyclic graph with non-negative weights assigned to edges [7]. To build an acyclic graph, we consider all the paths from the loop header H to its natural latch L.

Once we have determined – statically – the cost of a loop iteration, we instrument it. To this end, we create a counter variable at the loop's header, and increment it by the estimated cost. Notice that incrementing this counter at the loop header will account for one more iteration than the real execution. Nevertheless, it will not affect our cost analysis. We chose to do it like this because the loop header is unique, and is always executed, independent on the way the

```
1   void search(char** book, int N, int M) {
2     for (i = 0; i < N; i++) {
3       char* line = book[i];
4       for (j = 0; j < M; j++) {
5         if (line[j] == '\0') {
6           break;
7         } else {
8           match(line, pattern);
9         }
10      }
11    }
12  }
```

(a)

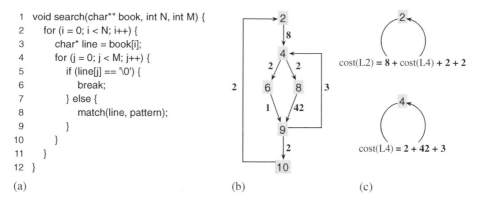

(b)   (c)

Fig. 5. (a) Program with a multi-path loop. (b) The cost-graph of the program. Nodes represent program points and the edges' weights represent the number of executed instructions between two points. (c) The cost of each loop iteration.

program flows within the loop body. Figure 5 (c) shows the cost expressions that we create for each loop. In the figure, edges represent paths within the loop, and the nodes are the headers of those loops. Each one of these values is added once per iteration of the loop. Once we have instrumented the program, we execute it. As mentioned before, each execution of an instrumented program outputs the values of each loop input, together with the number of operations executed within that loop.

3.4   Polynomial Interpolation

We log the output of our profiler and parse it to extract pairs: input value × execution cost. With these points, we execute a polynomial interpolation method to find the curve that best fits into this set. Our interpolation works as follows: we test different polynomials, starting from a line (degree 1) upwards until $n - 1$, where n is the number of points available. At step i we need $i + 1$ points to determine a polynomial. Any group of $i + 1$ different points fits this purpose. We call this group of points the *guiding set*. We use the points that are left to check if we have found the correct polynomial. These remaining points are called the *verification set*. We stop interpolation if, upon finding a polynomial p, of degree k, $k < n - 1$, we notice that the $n - k$ points in the verification set fit perfectly into p. Our interpolation only works for single-variable polynomials, but we can infer the complexity of nests of loops by multiplying symbolically their individual complexities.

   Figure 6 illustrates this process for the program seen in Fig. 1. The figure has two blocks of loops; thus, we produce two polynomials. Let us take a deeper look into the polynomial that we produce for the loop that exists at lines 18–25 of Fig. 1. This curve is shown in Fig. 6(a). In this example, we assume that we have obtained, after profiling the program with eight different inputs, the following pairs of size × cost: (13, 183), (50, 2,551), (72, 5,257), (80, 6,481),

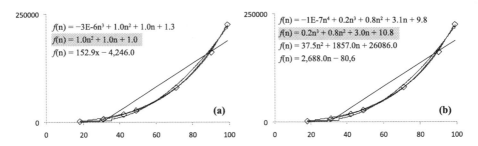

Fig. 6. (a) Polynomials found for the loop at lines 18–25 of Fig. 1. (b) Polynomials found for the loop nest at lines 7–15. In each figure, the first curve that fits the points in the verification set is marked in gray.

(98, 9,704), (115, 13,341), (139, 19,461). To derive a polynomial that describes the complexity of this loop, we try to interpolate a line across those points using, as our guiding set, only the first two pairs, e.g., (13, 183) and (50, 2,551). This line does not contain the other six points, which form the verification set. Thus, we move on to try a polynomial of degree two, this time, adding also the pair (72, 5,257) to our guiding set. The new polynomial, $n^2 + n + 0.8$ contains the points in our verification set. Hence, we let it denote the computational cost of the loop. The complexity of the loop is then $O(n^2)$, where n is the only symbolic input of the loop under analysis, as we have explained in Sect. 3.1. We perform similar process to discover the polynomial that characterizes the loop nest at lines 7–15 of Fig. 1. However, this time our search stabilizes in a third-degree polynomial. Figure 6(b) shows this curve.

4   Experiments

To examine the real applicability of our technique, we have implemented it as a prototype tool. We have used the LLVM compilation infrastructure to perform the static analysis and code instrumentation phases mentioned in Sects. 3.1–3.3. All the experiments that we shall present in this section have been run on an Intel Xeon processor, with 16 GB of RAM, running Linux Ubuntu. The main goals of these experiments are: (1) to find out how effective is the technique when applied to the loops found in real-world programs; and (2) to provide a taxonomy of the loops found in real-world systems.

Effectiveness. To achieve our first goal – to probe the effectiveness of our tool – we have executed it on the Polybench [19] and Rodinia [3] benchmark suites. We have checked, manually, the answers produced by our tool for every loop in these benchmarks. This exercise shows that we are able to correctly analyze 99.7 % of the loops in Polybench. The remaining 0.3 % is due to a single loop which is constant for the first two points, and varies for larger inputs. This behavior makes it impossible for us to get a perfect polynomial match. For Rodinia – a much bigger and general benchmark suite – our tool correctly analysed 63.58 %

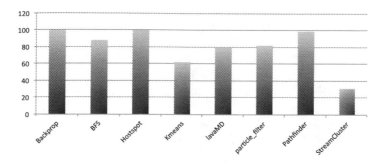

Fig. 7. Percentage of loops per benchmark of Rodinia that we could analyze. The correctness of all these results have been checked manually.

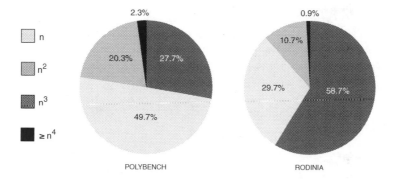

Fig. 8. Distribution of complexities. In this chart we ignore the difference between variables - we consider that $n \times m$ is equals to n^2, for instance.

of the loops. However, the execution flow never reached some functions during our profiling phase so we could not generate data for them. If we ignore those functions, our success rate increases to 69.18 %.

Our results are worse for Rodinia because of three reasons: (1) some loops are not polynomial, but we use a polynomial interpolation; (2) some loops iterate over structures that our technique does not handle, such as strings or files; and (3) some loops have 3 or 4 inputs that bound their execution. In this case, we do not generate pairs of input vs time for the loop. Figure 7 shows the percentage of loops that we could analyze per Rodinia benchmark. We do not show a chart for Polybench, because we believe that this chart is not interesting. It would have almost only bars at 100 % of precision.

Given all the machinery that we now have in place, we thought that it would be interesting to categorize the loop nests that we have found in our benchmarks. Figure 8 shows the distribution of complexities found in both benchmark suites. The majority of loop nests in Rodinia are linear, and only a handful of them are $O(N^4)$ or higher. In Polybench, the picture is slightly different. Most of the loop nests in that collection are quadratic. This happens because Polybench has been designed to test optimizations built over the polytope model. Linear loops

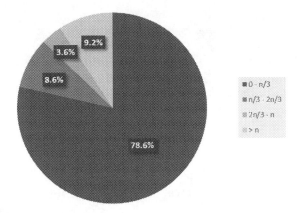

Fig. 9. Quality of the approximation heuristic seen in Sect. 3.3. Each slice groups a range of loops for which our approximation yielded similar results. For instance, for 78.6 % of the loops the approximation yields a result that is within $[0, 1/3]$ of the observed value.

are simply not challenging enough to the current state-of-the-art polyhedron techniques.

The Topology of Loops. To better understand the power and limitations of the technique that we advocate in this paper, we chose to analyze in greater detail the topology of loops found in real-world programs. In addition to Rodinia and Polybench, this time we chose to study also the loops present in SPEC CPU 2006, to have a larger body of samples.

We have counted the number of independent loops within functions. We say that two loops, L_1 and L_2, are independent if one is not nested within the other. We saw that 21.8 % of the functions have at least two independent loops in Polybench, 40.4 % in Rodinia, and 38.1 % in SPEC. These numbers let us conclude that it is important, from a software engineering point of view, to output complexity results in a finer grain than functions, as aprof does. We do it at the loop level. This finer granularity gives developers more information to understand a function's behaviour. We have also counted the number of loops that are executed conditionally within a function. We found 92 control-flow breaks (e.g. returns or exit calls) in the 99 functions that we have analyzed. This data shows that if we ignore conditional execution, then we may output incomplete – or incorrect – results. That is why we use the *expander* operator.

The last metric that we have studied is the number of loops with multiple paths. We saw that 51.2 % of the loops in SPEC have multiple paths. We also would like to know how far from the exact number of instructions we stay when using the approximation seen in Sect. 3.3. In that case, we approximate the cost of a loop as the cost of its longest path. By profiling the actual number of instructions executed in our benchmarks, we got that, most of the time, our approximation is within 33 % of the actual result. This metric shows that using the heuristic from Sect. 3.3 increases the applicability of our analysis without compromising its results. Figure 9 shows a distribution of how distant our approximation is from the real program behavior.

5   Related Works

Recent work has attempted to improve the state of the art on complexity analysis. Particularly, profiler-based approaches have been able to give interesting results. Goldsmith *et al.* [9] proposed a technique which consists in executing the target program over workloads with different orders of magnitude and tracking how many times each program location was executed. They use polynomial regression to fit the data into a linear or power-law model. However, the user has to specify, for each workload, the value of features - a feature is an input property which affects the algorithm execution, e.g. the size of an array or the height of a tree. Our technique is able to automatically infer loops' inputs; hence, it does not require this type of user intervention.

Zaparanuks *et al.* [22] proposed the concept of algorithmic profiler. Their approach consists in grouping the basic blocks of a loop and the functions which make a cycle in the call-graph into the so called *repetition nodes*. Those nodes are then combined in units that they have named *algorithms*. The technique is able to identify if an algorithm is modifying or traversing a list or an array, for example. In order to estimate the complexity of an algorithm, they retrieve the size of the inputs and some performance metrics for each execution of the repetition nodes. This modus operandi leads to a significant overhead, since the analyzer iterates over the entire data structure to calculate its size. The automatic reconstruction of data-structures is still an incipient area of research. Therefore, Zaparanuks *et al.* have implemented a prototype which, up to this point, can analyze only toy examples. We cannot reconstruct recursive data-structures as Zaparanuks does; however, our approach is able to infer the complexity of most of the loops in a real-world benchmark suite.

The work that is the most related to ours is Coppa *et al.*'s input sensitive profiler [4]. This work has materialized itself into `aprof` tool. Core to `aprof`'s work is the notion of Read Memory Size (RMS). This metric represents the number of memory locations which are read before they have been written inside a function. Aprof was implemented as a *Valgrind* [17] extension. We believe that `aprof` is the most practical tool available nowadays to infer the complexity of general purpose programs. Nevertheless, it has the shortcomings which we have described in Sect. 1: (i) the granularity of results is at the function, not at the loop, level; (ii) users have to fit equation by hand in `aprof`'s results to find the complexity of a function; and (iii) results are given in terms of RMS, which may not be significant to the developer. Our technique is capable of addressing these drawbacks.

There exists a plethora of work related to the static estimation of complexity of code [1,5,11,13,16]. Our work is essentially different from these approaches, because our results are based on program behavior observed at runtime. In other words, our approach is dynamic: we execute and profile the program to infer its computational complexity. The downside of our approach is that we are not able to *prove* properties about the program's complexity: there are no guarantees that we will be able to observe every possible execution path within the program code. The upside is precision: our approach is able to reason about typical programming language features such as dynamically allocated memory, multiple paths in loops, non-structured control flow graphs and pointer arithmetics. So far, these real-world constructs have been challenging adversaries to the purely static analyses.

6 Conclusion

This paper has presented a new technique, based on a combination of profiling and static analysis, to infer the complexity of code. Static analysis gives us the names of variables that bound the trip count of loops. Profiling lets us associate these variables with the number of operations in the loops that they control. We believe that our approach, whenever applicable, yields results that are more meaningful to the application developer than the state-of-the-art tools that are currently available. A tool that implements the technique is publicly available[1] for use. There are several ways in which such a tool can be employed. Our immediate goal is to use it to help in the automatic placement of code in non-uniform memory access architectures. In this scenario, it is worthwhile to migrate processes of high computational cost closer to the memory banks that contain the data that said processes use. A totally static solution has been devised to this problem by Piccoli *et al.* [18]. Our intention is to add to this solution a dynamic component based on this paper's ideas, in hopes to increase its precision.

References

1. Alves, P.R.O., Rodrigues, R.E., de Souza, R.M., Pereira, F.M.Q.: A case for a fast trip count predictor. Inf. Process. Lett. **115**(2), 146–150 (2015)
2. Appel, A.W., Palsberg, J.: Modern Compiler Implementation in Java, 2nd edn. Cambridge University Press, Cambridge (2002)
3. Che, S., Boyer, M., Meng, J., Tarjan, D., Sheaffer, J.W., Lee, S.-H., Skadron, K.: Rodinia: a benchmark suite for heterogeneous computing. In: IISWC, pp. 44–54. IEEE (2009)
4. Coppa, E., Demetrescu, C., Finocchi, I.: Input-sensitive profiling. In: PLDI. ACM (2012)
5. Danielsson, N.A.: Lightweight semiformal time complexity analysis for purely functional data structures. In: POPL, pp. 133–144. ACM (2008)
6. Debray, S.K., Lin, N.-W.: Cost analysis of logic programs. ACM Trans. Program. Lang. Syst. **15**(5), 826–875 (1993)
7. Dijkstra, E.W.: A note on two problems in connexion with graphs. Numer. Math. **1**, 269–271 (1959)

---

[1] http://demontiejr.github.io/asymptus.

8. Ferrante, J., Ottenstein, K.J., Warren, J.D.: The program dependence graph and its use in optimization. TOPLAS **9**(3), 319–349 (1987)
9. Goldsmith, S.F., Aiken, A.S., Wilkerson, D.S.: Measuring empirical computational complexity. In: FSE, pp. 395–404. ACM (2007)
10. Graham, S.L., Kessler, P.B., McKusick, M.K.: gprof: a call graph execution profiler (with retrospective). In: Best of PLDI, pp. 49–57 (1982)
11. Gulavani, B.S., Gulwani, S.: A numerical abstract domain based on *expression abstraction* and *max operator* with application in timing analysis. In: Gupta, A., Malik, S. (eds.) CAV 2008. LNCS, vol. 5123, pp. 370–384. Springer, Heidelberg (2008)
12. Gulwani, S., Jain, S., Koskinen, E.: Control-flow refinement and progress invariants for bound analysis. In: PLDI, pp. 375–385. ACM (2009)
13. Gulwani, S., Mehra, K.K., Chilimbi, T.: SPEED: precise and efficient static estimation of program computational complexity. In: POPL, pp. 127–139. ACM (2009)
14. Lattner, C., Adve, V.S.: LLVM: a compilation framework for lifelong program analysis & transformation. In: CGO, pp. 75–88. IEEE (2004)
15. Le Métayer, D.: Ace: an automatic complexity evaluator. ACM Trans. Program. Lang. Syst. **10**(2), 248–266 (1988)
16. Monniaux, D., Gonnord, L.: Using bounded model checking to focus fixpoint iterations. In: Yahav, E. (ed.) Static Analysis. LNCS, vol. 6887, pp. 369–385. Springer, Heidelberg (2011)
17. Nethercote, N., Seward, J.: Valgrind: a framework for heavyweight dynamic binary instrumentation. In: PLDI, pp. 89–100. ACM (2007)
18. Piccoli, G., Santos, H., Rodrigues, R., Pousa, C., Borin, E., Pereira, F.M.Q.: Compiler support for selective page migration in NUMA architectures. In: PACT, pp. 369–380. ACM (2014)
19. Pouchet, L.-N.: Polybench: the polyhedral benchmark suite (2012). http://www.cs.ucla.edu/pouchet/software/polybench/. Accessed April 2015
20. Wegbreit, B.: Mechanical program analysis. Commun. ACM **18**(9), 528–539 (1975)
21. Wolfe, M.: High Performance Compilers for Parallel Computing, 1st edn. Adison-Wesley, Redwood City (1996)
22. Zaparanuks, D., Hauswirth, M.: Algorithmic profiling. In: PLDI, pp. 67–76. ACM (2012)

Type Inference for GADTs and Anti-unification

Adelaine Gelain[1], Cristiano Vasconcellos[1]([✉]),
Carlos Camarão[2], and Rodrigo Ribeiro[3]

[1] DCC, Universidade do Estado de Santa Catarina (UDESC), Joinville, Brazil
adelainegelain@gmail.com, cristiano.vasconcellos@udesc.br
[2] DCC, Universidade Federal de Minas Gerais (UFMG), Belo Horizonte, Brazil
camarao@dcc.ufmg.br
[3] DECSI, Universidade Federal de Ouro Preto (UFOP), João Monlevade, Brazil
rodrigo@decsi.ufop.br

Abstract. Nowadays the support of generalized algebraic data types (GADTs) in extensions of Haskell allows functions defined over GADTs to be written without the need for type annotations in some cases and requires type annotations in other cases. In this paper we present a type inference algorithm for GADTs that is based on a closed-world approach to overloading and uses anti-unification and constraint-set satisfiability to infer the relationship between the types of function arguments and result. Through some examples, we show how the proposed algorithm allows more functions defined over GADTs to be written without the need for type annotations.

1 Introduction

Generalized Algebraic Data Types (*GADTs*) constitute a powerful extension to algebraic data types of functional languages like Haskell and ML, and are nowadays widely used. A GADT is defined by giving an explicit type signature for each of its constructors. This allows functions to be defined by specifying equations that return expressions of distinct types, all instances of the GADT type. For example, the function *eval*, presented in e.g. [7,12], evaluates an expression and returns a value of a type that varies according to the argument type (due to space reasons the *Term* constructor is presented in a shortened form):

```
data Term a where
     Lit   ::  Int → Term Int
     Inc   ::  Term Int → Term Int
     IsZ   ::  Term Int → Term Bool
     If    ::  Term Bool → Term a → Term a → Term a
     Pair  ::  Term a → Term b → Term (a,b)
```

A. Pardo and S.D. Swierstra (Eds.): SBLP 2015, LNCS 9325, pp. 16–30, 2015.
DOI: 10.1007/978-3-319-24012-1_2

```
eval  ::  Term  a → a
eval  (Lit i)      = i
eval  (Inc t)      = 1 + eval t
eval  (IsZ i)      = 0 == eval i
eval  (If l e1 e2) = if eval l then eval e1 else eval e2
eval  (Pair a b)   = (eval a, eval b)
```

The use of an algebraic data type would destroy the simplicity of the evaluator, by requiring a declaration of another algebraic data type with a distinct constructor (tag) for each possible distinct type of the result, with undesirable constructor tagging and untagging.

Type inference with GADTs is complex, mainly because of problems in identifying a principal type in many cases. Consider the following example, taken from [15]:

```
data T a where
   T1 :: Int → T Bool
   T2 :: T a

test (T1 n) _ = n > 0
test T2     r = r
```

In the first alternative of *test*, the result type inferred for the expression $n > 0$, *Bool*, is associated with the type of constructor $T1$, and $(T1\ n)$ can be determined to have type $T\ Bool$, with n of type *Int*. In the second alternative of *test*, there is no explicit association between type $T\ a$, constructed by the use of $T2$, and the return type (the type of r), and thus in this case the type of the result should be unified with that of the first alternative (*Bool*). A relation between the GADT type and the type of the result could exist, and be explicitly annotated: the following type signatures are both accepted for the function *test*, but none is an instance of the other:

$$test :: \forall a.\ T\ a\ \rightarrow\ Bool\ \rightarrow\ Bool$$
$$test :: \forall a.\ T\ a\ \rightarrow\ a\ \rightarrow\ a$$

Several approaches have been proposed to deal with type inference for GADTs, most of them imposing several restrictions. GADTs are supported in GHC 7.10.1 [20] as described in [6], where type checking is based on type signatures explicitly given by the programmer. Recent work [15,22] describes a type inference algorithm that can avoid type signatures in a restricted number of cases.

In this article we present another type inferencing algorithm that accepts the declaration of functions based on GADTs without the need for type signatures (Sect. 3). Examples where types can and cannot be inferred, and issues related to the existence or not of principal types, are also discussed in Sect. 3.

Our type inference algorithm uses anti-unification (defined in Sect. 2.1) to capture the relation between the types of the alternatives. Type variables that are not related to GADTs are unified as usual. Cases involving recursive calls can be polymorphic recursive, and are handled as if each alternative is an overloaded definition. In this case, a constraint is added to the type of the recursive call. Constraint-set satisfiability of these constraints is used to construct a substitution that is used for instantiating the type of the alternative, in a process similar to the handling of overloading in System CT [2]. A brief review of System CT is given in Sect. 2.

2 Preliminaries

In this section we introduce some basic definitions and notations. We consider that meta-variables defined can appear primed or subscripted.

Meta-variable usage is defined in the paper as follows: x, y denote term variables, C, D data constructors, α, β ($a, b, \ldots$ in examples) type variables, T a type constructor, e a term, τ, ρ simple types, κ a constraint set, $x : \tau$ a constraint, σ a type, Γ a typing context, that is, a set of pairs written as $x : \sigma$, and S a substitution.

The notation $\overline{a}^n$, or simply $\overline{a}$, denotes the sequence $a_1, \ldots, a_n$, where $n \geq 0$. When used in a context of a set, it denotes the corresponding set of elements in the sequence $\{a_1, \ldots, a_n\}$.

A substitution is a function from type variables to simple type expressions (cf. Sect. 3.2). The identity substitution denoted by id. $S\sigma$ represents the capture-free operation of substituting $S(\alpha)$ for each free occurrence of α in σ.

We overload the substitution application on constraints, constraint sets and sets of types. Definition of application on these elements is straightforward. The symbol $\circ$ denotes function composition and $dom(S) = \{\alpha \mid S(\alpha) \neq \alpha\}$.

The notation $S[\overline{\alpha} \mapsto \overline{\tau}]$ denotes the updating of S such that $\overline{\alpha}$ maps to $\overline{\tau}$, that is, the substitution S' such that $S'(\beta) = \tau_i$ if $\beta = \alpha_i$, for $i = 1, ..., n$, otherwise $S(\beta)$. Also, $[\overline{\alpha} \mapsto \overline{\tau}] = id[\overline{\alpha} \mapsto \overline{\tau}]$.

2.1 Anti-unification

A type τ is a generalization — also called (first-order) *anti-unification* [3] — of simple types $\overline{\tau}^n$ if there exist substitutions $\overline{S}^n$ such that $S_i(\tau) = \tau_i$, for $i = 1, \ldots, n$.

We call a function that gives the least generalization of a finite set of simple types the *least common generalization (lcg)*.

An algorithm for computing the *lcg* of a finite set of types in presented in Fig. 1. The concept of least common generalization was studied by Gordon Plotkin [10,11], that defined a function for constructing a generalization of two symbolic expressions.

$$lcg(\mathbb{T}) = \tau \quad \textsf{where } (\tau, S) = lcg'(\mathbb{T}, \emptyset), \textsf{ for some } S$$

$$lcg'(\{\tau\}, S) = (\tau, S)$$

$$lcg'(\{\tau_1, \tau_2\} \cup \mathbb{T}, S) = lcg''(\tau, \tau', S') \quad \textsf{where } \begin{aligned}(\tau, S_0) &= lcg''(\tau_1, \tau_2, S)\\ (\tau', S') &= lcg'(\mathbb{T}, S_0)\end{aligned}$$

$$lcg''(C \, \overline{\tau}^{\,n}, D \, \overline{\rho}^{\,m}, S) =$$
$$\quad \textsf{if } S(\alpha) = (C \, \overline{\tau}^{\,n}, D \, \overline{\rho}^{\,m}) \textsf{ for some } \alpha \textsf{ then } (\alpha, S)$$
$$\quad \textsf{else}$$
$$\qquad \textsf{if } n \neq m \textsf{ then } (\beta, S[\beta \mapsto (C \, \overline{\tau}^{\,n}, D \, \overline{\rho}^{\,m})])$$
$$\qquad\quad \textsf{where } \beta \textsf{ is a fresh type variable}$$
$$\qquad \textsf{else } (\psi \, \overline{\tau'}^{\,n}, S_n)$$
$$\qquad\quad \textsf{where } (\psi, S_0) = \begin{cases} (C, S) & \textsf{if } C = D \\ (\alpha, S[\alpha \mapsto (C, D)]) & \textsf{otherwise, } \alpha \textsf{ is fresh} \end{cases}$$
$$\qquad\qquad\quad (\tau'_i, S_i) = lcg''(\tau_i, \rho_i, S_{i-1}), \textsf{ for } i = 1, \ldots, n$$

Fig. 1. Least common generalization

2.2 System CT

System CT is an extension of the Damas-Milner type system for dealing with overloading [1,2,13,14]. Our initial view for the definition of system CT was to consider a simple extension where a name (or symbol) could have more than one type assumption in a typing context. This led to the adoption of a closed world approach for overloading [1,2,21]. However for efficiency reasons, we have changed our initial idea about the support of only a closed world approach to overloading, due to the need (in a closed world) of checking constraint-set satisfiability for each function application. Nowadays, our view, highly influenced by Haskell's open world approach, is that an open world is the preferred approach for supporting overloading. We leave discussion of an optional, instead of mandatory, use of type classes, as well as a related motivation for changing Haskell's ambiguity rule, to future work.

The principal type of overloaded symbols is defined in system CT by computing the anti-unification of the types of the available definitions of these symbols in the typing context, instead of requiring them to be explicitly annotated in a class declaration.

The least common generalization of the finite set of types of the definitions of an overloaded symbol in a given context is taken as the (principal) type of the overloaded symbol. In system CT a type is denoted by $\forall \bar{\alpha}. \, \kappa. \, \tau$, where κ is a possibly empty constraint set and τ is a simple type (i.e. an unconstrained and unquantified type). A constraint in system CT is a pair $x : \tau$, where x is an overloaded symbol and τ is a simple type. For example, a typing context, $\Gamma_{==}$, in which the equality symbol is overloaded with types *Int* and *Char* contains the following type assumptions:

$$(\texttt{==}) : Int \rightarrow Int \rightarrow Bool$$
$$(\texttt{==}) : Char \rightarrow Char \rightarrow Bool$$

In this case, the principal type of (==) in $\Gamma_{\texttt{==}}$ is obtained by the least common generalization of the two types of (==) in this typing context, and is given by:

$$\forall a.\{(\texttt{==}):a \rightarrow a \rightarrow Bool\}.\, a \rightarrow a \rightarrow Bool$$

Constraint (==) : $a \rightarrow a \rightarrow Bool$ on this type is similar to Haskell's constraint *Eq a*, where such type of (==) is annotated, the difference being essentially the abscence of a constraint on (/=) that is also available in type class *Eq*. The purpose of the constraint is the same as in Haskell: in this case, to allow instantiation of type variable *a* in $\Gamma_{\texttt{==}}$ only for types *Int* and *Char*. Type inference in system *CT* is a process similar to type inference in Haskell. In particular, the use of overloaded symbols in expressions for which overloading is not resolved causes a constraint to be included in the inferred type. For example, consider:

```
insert  a  []       = [a]
insert  a  (b:x)
    | a == b        = b:x
    | otherwise     = b: insert  a  x
```

The type of *insert* in this typing context is inferred to be:

$$insert :: \ \forall a.\,\{(\texttt{==}) : a \rightarrow a \rightarrow Bool\}.\, a \rightarrow [a] \rightarrow [a]$$

In general, in a constrained type $\forall \bar{a}^n.\kappa.\tau$, κ is a set of constraints that restricts the set of types to which $\forall \bar{a}^n.\tau$ may be instantiated: every instance must be such that the resulting constraint set must be satisfiable in the relevant typing context. Constraint set satisfiability is in general an undecidable problem [16,17], but it can be made decidable without significantly affecting the set of typeable programs [14]. See also [2,4,5,18].

During type inference, the substitution returned by the function — called *sat* — that computes a substitution that verifies (proves) satisfiability of a given constraint set in a given typing context — or, equivalently, that verifies whether the constraint set is entailed by a set of constraints on the types of definitions of symbols in the typing context — can be used to "improve" the constrained type. See e.g. [5,13,14] for definitions of *sat* and for the problem of constraint-set satisfiability (CS-SAT).

In a closed world, the substitution returned by *sat* is needed to improve the type of recursive functions. For example, consider the inference of the principal type of overloaded equality for lists, in context $\Gamma_{(\texttt{==})}$:

$$
\begin{aligned}
\texttt{[]} \quad\quad &\texttt{==}\ \texttt{[]} \quad\quad = \textit{True} \\
(a:x) \ &\texttt{==}\ (b:y) = a\ \texttt{==}\ b\ \texttt{\&\&}\ x\ \texttt{==}\ y \\
\_ \quad\quad\ &\texttt{==}\ \_ \quad\quad = \textit{False}
\end{aligned}
$$

The (principal) type of (==) is inferred by considering firstly the types of (==) used in the recursive definition, initially given by:

$$\{(\texttt{==}) : a \to b \to Bool, (\texttt{==}) : [a] \to [b] \to Bool\}.\ [a] \to [b] \to Bool \qquad (1)$$

The first constraint on the type above comes from $a\ \texttt{==}\ b$, and the second from $x\texttt{==}y$. Note that the type of (==) cannot be inferred from the lcg of the types of (==) in the typing context, because a new definition is being given, and this in general will modify the lcg. Function sat comes to the rescue, being able to compute a substitution that is used to improve the type of (==) to:

$$\forall a.\{(\texttt{==}) : a \to a \to Bool\}.\ [a] \to [a] \to Bool$$

despite the existence of an infinite set of substitutions that can be used to instantiate the type (1) above:

$$
\begin{aligned}
\{\{a \mapsto Int, b \mapsto Int\}, \{a \mapsto Char, b \mapsto Char\}, \{a \mapsto [Int], b \mapsto [Int]\}, \{a \mapsto [Char], \\
\{b \mapsto [Char]\}, \{a \mapsto [[Int]], b \mapsto [[Int]]\}, \{a \mapsto [[Char]], b \mapsto [[Char]]\}, \dots\}
\end{aligned}
$$

The sat algorithm is defined in [2,14].

Type inference for polymorphic recursion is treated in a similar way.

3   Type Inference

Let's say that a GADT function is a function such that the type of a parameter or of the result is a GADT type. Type inference of a GADT function involves, in our approach, the generalization of the types used in the defining alternatives. The substitution returned by sat is used to improve the inferred type, using a process of type inference that has the following phases:

1. The type of each defining alternative is inferred, with a constraint (included in the constraint set) for each recursive use of the GADT function.
2. The type of each equation j is improved by the substitution given by $sat(\kappa_j, \Gamma)$, where κ_j is the constraint set on the type inferred for equation j and Γ contains the type assumptions of used overloaded symbols together with the set $\{x : \sigma_i \mid i = 1, \dots, n\}$, where x is the name being defined and σ_i is the type of the i-th equation in the definition of x that is not recursively defined.
3. Compute the lcg of the simple type of the alternatives.
4. Compute the substitution that is the most general unifier of the types of alternatives of the GADT function which do not involve a GADT constructor and apply this substitution to obtain the type of each alternative.

We present next some examples that illustrate the type inference process.

3.1 Examples

Example 1. Type Inference of function *test*

The types inferred for each alternative of the function *test*, presented in Sect. 1, are:

$$
\begin{aligned}
test \;&::\; T\ Bool \rightarrow a \rightarrow Bool \\
test \;&::\; T\ b \quad\;\; \rightarrow c \rightarrow c
\end{aligned}
$$

In cases such as this, where recursive calls do not occur, no restriction is generated, making the call to *sat* unnecessary. The *lcg* is then computed, taking the set of types of the alternatives as a parameter. The type obtained by *lcg* allows observation of the dependency that exists between the types of each alternative with those of the generalized type: types for which there is no association with the type of a GADT are unified. The generalization of the types of the alternatives in the definition of the function *test* yields:

$$
test \;::\; T\ b' \rightarrow c' \rightarrow d'
$$

Now, b' is associated with a GADT, and c', d' are not. Thus, phase (4) above specifies that a and c should be unified, as well as *Bool* and c, resulting in:

$$
test \;::\; \forall a.\, T\ a \rightarrow Bool \;\rightarrow Bool
$$

As discussed in Sect. 1, type $\forall a.\, T\, a \rightarrow a \rightarrow a$ could also serve as the type of *test*, and in that case expression (*test T2* 'a') would be type-correct.

In Haskell, type inference for the function *test* generates *implication constraints* [15,22], given by (where $\sim$ is a type equality constraint and $\supset$ denotes an implication constraint):

$$
(a \sim T\ b) \wedge (b \sim Bool \supset c \sim Bool) \wedge (a \sim T\ d) \wedge (c \sim e)
$$

Type equality constraint ($b \sim Bool$) is generated from $T1\ n$, type equality constraint ($c \sim Bool$) is generated from the first alternative in the definition of *test*, type equality constraint ($c \sim e$) from the second alternative in the definition of *test*, where e is the type of r, which is in this case free to be unified ($\{e \mapsto c\}$). The meaning of an implication constraint can be understood by considering that, in this example, ($b \sim Bool \supset c \sim Bool$) indicates that if type variable b is instantiated to *Bool* then so must c. These constraints have substitution $\{c \mapsto Bool\}$ as a solution. Application of this substitution on the type of *test* yields type $T\ b \rightarrow Bool \;\rightarrow Bool$, which is the same type inferred by our algorithm. However, type variable c is considered *untouchable* in the implication constraint, and then type inference fails. Type variables which occur in implication constraints are considered untouchable within these constraints, and can only be substituted as a result of applying substitutions obtained as a result of solving other constraints. In GHC 7.6.x type inference proceeds as outlined, but from version 7.8.1 a more restricted set of GADT functions for non-annotated types was adopted.

Example 2. Type Inference of function *eval*

In the definition of *eval*, presented in Sect. 1, recursive calls involving polymorphic recursion occur in some alternatives, while the type of *eval* has not been inferred yet. To handle such cases, constraints are generated from the type required for each recursive call. These constraints are subsequently used in the type improvement process.

The alternative with pattern on constructor *If* has recursive calls for all arguments of the constructor (l, $e1$ and $e1$). l has type *Term Bool*, and $e1, e2$ have type *Term a*. Constraints $\{eval : Term\ a \to b, eval : Term\ Bool \to Bool\}$ are generated, and the type of the alternative is inferred also as *Term $a \to b$*. Type inference for the constructor *Pair* proceeds in a similar way. The types inferred for each alternative are as follows:

$$
\begin{array}{lll}
(Lit\ i) & eval :: & Term\ Int \to Int \\
(Inc\ t) & eval :: & Term\ Int \to Int \\
(IsZ\ i) & eval :: & Term\ Bool \to Bool \\
(If\ l\ e1\ e2) & eval :: & \{eval : Term\ Bool \to Bool, \\
& & \quad eval : Term\ a \to b\}.\ Term\ a \to b \\
(Pair\ x\ y) & eval :: & \{eval : Term\ c \to e, \\
& & \quad eval : Term\ d \to f\}.\ Term\ (c,d) \to (e,f)
\end{array}
$$

After this, the types of the alternatives which contain constraints are subject to type improvement, which consists of the application of the substitution given by $sat(\kappa, \Gamma)$, where κ is the possibly empty constraint set in the type of each alternative and $\Gamma = \{eval : Term\ Int \to Int, eval : Term\ Bool \to Bool\}$. After type improvement the following types are inferred for each alternative:

$$
\begin{array}{lll}
(Lit\ i) & eval :: & Term\ Int \to Int \\
(Inc\ t) & eval :: & Term\ Int \to Int \\
(IsZ\ i) & eval :: & Term\ Bool \to Bool \\
(If\ l\ e1\ e2) & eval :: & Term\ a \to a \\
(Pair\ x\ y) & eval :: & Term\ (c,d) \to (c,d)
\end{array}
$$

The type inferred for *eval* is the *lcg* of the types of the alternatives, given by:

$$
eval :: \forall a.\ Term\ a \to a
$$

In this case, all types are associated with the GADT, what characterizes them as types that should not be unified, and, as in this case all types are associated to the GADT, we have that, in this case, the type inferred is the principal type.

Example 3. In some cases anti-unification does not capture the relationship between types of alternatives. Consider for example the following function, presented in [18]:

$$
\begin{aligned}
&\textbf{data } \textit{Erk} \ a \ b \ \textbf{where} \\
&\quad I \ :: \ \textit{Int} \rightarrow \ \textbf{Erk} \ \textit{Int} \ b \\
&\quad B \ :: \ \textit{Bool} \rightarrow \ \textbf{Erk} \ a \ \textit{Bool}
\end{aligned}
$$

$$
\begin{aligned}
&f \ (I \ a) = a + 1 \\
&f \ (B \ b) = b \ \&\& \ \textit{True}
\end{aligned}
$$

The generalization of the types of the alternatives in the definition of f is: $Erk \ a \ b \rightarrow c$. Since type variable c is not associated to a GADT, types Int and $Bool$ are unified, causing the definition of f to be rejected. However, for example with annotated type $Erk \ a \ a \rightarrow a$ this function can be given a proper type.

3.2   Term and Type Syntax

The context-free syntax of terms and types is presented in Fig. 2. For simplicity and following common practice, kinds are not considered in type expressions and type expressions which are not simple types are not explicitly distinguished from simple types. Type expression variables are called simply type variables. There is a distinguished type constructor that is written as an infix operator, $\tau \rightarrow \tau'$, as usual.

Terms	$e ::= x \mid C \mid \lambda x.e \mid e\,e' \mid \textbf{let } x = e \textbf{ in } e' \mid \textbf{case } e \textbf{ of } \overline{C\,\overline{x} \rightarrow e}$
Simple types	$\tau ::= \alpha\,\overline{\tau} \mid T\,\overline{\tau}$
Type schemes	$\sigma ::= \forall\overline{\alpha}.\kappa.\tau$

Fig. 2. Syntax of terms and types

We use the following operations over typing contexts:

$$
\begin{aligned}
\Gamma(x) &= \{\sigma \mid x : \sigma \in \Gamma\} \\
\Gamma, x : \sigma &= (\Gamma - \{x : \sigma \mid \ \sigma \in \Gamma(x)\}) \cup \{x : \sigma\}
\end{aligned}
$$

We let: (i) $tv(\sigma)$ denote the set of free type variables in σ, (ii) $gtv(\sigma)$ denote the set of free type variables that occur in the type of a GADT type constructor, (iii) $gtc(\tau)$ represent the set of GADT type constructors occurring in τ and (iv) $rtv(\tau)$ denote the set of free type variables that occur in the type of a recursive algebraic data type, such as lists and trees (the set $rtv(\tau)$ is used to avoid skolemization of type variables that occur in the type of the result of a generalized GADT function).

We use constraints to express a relationship between the return type of a function and its parameters, in case the type of parameters have a GADT constructor.

We also use the following notation to return the sets of constraints that contain types that mention GADT constructors:

$$\kappa_x^\star = \{x : \tau \in \kappa \mid gtc(\tau) \neq \emptyset\}$$

3.3 Algorithm Definition

For simplicity, we consider a language that is essentially core-ML extended with GADT functions — that is, we do not include inference of types of expressions with overloaded symbols. Readers interested in type inference for overloading are referred to [13].

The proposed algorithm is defined as a syntax-directed proof system, using formulas of the form $\Delta \mid \Gamma \vdash e : (\kappa.\tau, S)$, where Δ is an environment of names of recursive function definitions that contains constraints to be used in the process of type improvement for case branches involving GADTs, $\kappa.\tau$ is the type inferred for e and S is a substitution (used to instantiate type variables for obtaining type $\kappa.\tau$). Notation $\delta(x, \tau, \Delta)$ associates, with a symbol x and a type τ, constraint set $\{x : \tau\}$, if x is a recursively defined symbol, otherwise an empty constraint set. It is defined as:

$$\delta(x, \tau, \Delta) = \text{if } x \in \Delta \text{ then } \{x : \tau\} \text{ else } \emptyset$$

$$\frac{\Gamma(x) = \forall\overline{\alpha}.\,\tau' \quad \tau = [\overline{\alpha} \mapsto \overline{\beta}]\tau' \quad \overline{\beta} \text{ fresh}}{\Delta \mid \Gamma \vdash x : (\delta(x, \tau, \Delta).\,\tau, id)} \;\text{(VAR)}$$

$$\frac{\Delta \mid \Gamma, x : \alpha \vdash e : (\kappa.\tau, S) \quad \alpha \text{ fresh}}{\Delta \mid \Gamma \vdash \lambda x.e : (\kappa.\,S\,\alpha \to \tau, S)} \;\text{(LAM)}$$

$$\frac{\begin{array}{ll} \Delta \mid \Gamma \vdash e : (\kappa.\tau_1, S_1) & S' = unify(\{\tau_2 \to \alpha = \tau_1\}) \\ \Delta \mid S_1\,\Gamma \vdash e' : (\kappa'.\tau_2, S_2) & S = S' \circ S_2 \circ S_1 \quad \alpha \text{ fresh} \end{array}}{\Delta \mid \Gamma \vdash e\,e' : (S\,(\kappa \cup \kappa'.\alpha), S)} \;\text{(APP)}$$

$$\frac{\begin{array}{ll} \Delta, x \mid \Gamma \vdash e' : (\kappa_1.\tau_1, S_1) & \overline{\alpha} = tv(\kappa_1.\tau_1) - tv(\Gamma) \\ \Delta \mid \Gamma, x : \forall\overline{\alpha}.\tau_1 \vdash e : (\kappa_2.\tau_2, S_2) & S = S_2 \circ S_1 \end{array}}{\Delta \mid \Gamma \vdash \text{let } x = e' \text{ in } e : (S(\kappa_1 \cup \kappa_2.\tau_2), S)} \;\text{(LET)}$$

$$\frac{\begin{array}{c} \Delta \mid \Gamma \vdash e : (\kappa'.\tau', S) \quad \Delta \mid S\,\Gamma \vdash_{\text{alts}} (\{\overline{C\,\overline{x} \to e_1}\}, \tau') : \overline{(\kappa_i.\tau_i' \to \tau_i, S_i)} \\ S\,\Gamma \Vdash_x \overline{\kappa_i.\tau_i' \to \tau_i} \rightsquigarrow \tau' \to \tau \\ x \text{ name of GADT function with constructors } \overline{C} \end{array}}{\Delta \mid \Gamma \vdash \text{case } e \text{ of } \{\overline{C\,\overline{x} \to e_1}\} : (\tau, S)} \;\text{(CASE)}$$

Type inference rules are standard, with the exception of rules (VAR) and (CASE). The (VAR) rule generates a constraint for each symbol in Δ, used for improvement of types of GADT functions. Each variable x that is not in Δ has a type with an empty constraint set (remember that, for simplicity reasons, overloading is not treated in this paper). The (CASE) rule is the main part of the algorithm. First, the type of case scrutinee e is inferred. Then, the type of each case alternative is inferred (in the textual order, but the order is not relevant). Finally, if the case expression involves GADT constructors, the type of the case expression is improved, by using a separate type improvement judgement (since case alternatives are not expressions). Distinct case alternatives for the same constructor must be unified, but in this paper we consider for simplicity that each case alternative has a distinct constructor.

$$\frac{\Delta \mid \Gamma \vdash_{\texttt{alt}} (C\,\overline{x} \to e, T\,\overline{\tau'}) : (\kappa.T\,\overline{\tau'} \to \tau, S)}{\Delta \mid \Gamma \vdash_{\texttt{alts}} (\{C\,\overline{x} \to e\}, T\,\overline{\tau'}) : \{(\kappa.T\,\overline{\tau'} \to \tau, S)\}} \ \text{(ALTSEnd)}$$

$$\frac{\Delta \mid \Gamma \vdash_{\texttt{alts}} \overline{(C\,\overline{x'} \to e_1, T\,\overline{\tau'})} : \overline{(\kappa'.\tau_1, S_1)} \quad \Delta \mid \Gamma \vdash_{\texttt{alt}} (C\,\overline{x} \to e, T\,\overline{\tau'}) : (\kappa.T\,\overline{\tau'} \to \tau, S)}{\Delta \mid \Gamma \vdash_{\texttt{alts}} ((\{C\,\overline{x} \to e\} \cup \overline{C\,\overline{x'} \to e_1}), T\,\overline{\tau'}) : \{(\kappa.T\,\overline{\tau'} \to \tau, S)\} \cup \overline{(\kappa'.\tau_1, S_1)}} \ \text{(ALTSRec)}$$

$$\frac{\Gamma(C) = \forall \overline{\alpha}. \overline{\tau_1} \to T\,\overline{\tau_2}}{S' = \textit{unify}(\{T\,\overline{\tau_2} = T\,\overline{\tau'}\}) \quad \Delta \mid S'(\Gamma, \overline{x : \tau'}) \vdash e : (\kappa.\tau, S)}{\Delta \mid \Gamma \vdash_{\texttt{alt}} (C\,\overline{x} \to e, T\,\overline{\tau'}) : (\kappa.\,T\,\overline{\tau'} \to \tau, S)} \ \text{(ALT)}$$

In order to infer the type of a case alternative, we need to unify its constructor range type with the type inferred for the case scrutinee, producing a substitution that is used to instantiate the types of the parameters, and add them to the typing context to infer the type of the right-hand side of the alternative.

The judgement $\Gamma \Vdash_x \overline{(\kappa_i.\,\tau_i' \to \tau_i)} \leadsto (\tau' \to \tau, S)$ denotes the type improvement necessary for the inference of types of functions defined by pattern matching on a GADT function named x. Given a typing context Γ and, for each alternative i, a set of constrained types $\kappa_i.\tau_i' \to \tau_i$, type improvement yields the improved type $\tau' \to \tau$. Note that only functions that have alternatives with polymorphic recursion generate constraints. $sat(\kappa, \Gamma)$ computes the improvement substitution S for a set of constraints κ, using type assumptions given by Γ. This judgement uses function $specialize$ which computes a improvement substitution based on the types of the case alternatives and their generalization.

$$\begin{aligned} specialize(\tau, \emptyset) &= id \\ specialize(\tau, (\{\tau'\} \cup \mathbb{T})) &= \textit{unify}(\{\tau = \tau'\}) \circ specialize(\mathbb{T}) \end{aligned}$$

The type improvement judgement is defined as:

$$\frac{\overline{S_i = sat((\kappa_i)^\star_x, \{\overline{x : \tau_i' \to \tau_i}\} \cup \Gamma)}}{\tau_1 \to \tau_2 = lcg(\overline{S_i\,(\tau_i' \to \tau_i)}) \qquad \overline{K} \text{ are fresh Skolem constants}}{\overline{\alpha} = gtv(\tau_1) - rtv\,(\tau_2) \qquad S = specialize([\overline{\alpha} \mapsto \overline{K}](\tau_1 \to \tau_2), \overline{S_i\,(\tau_i' \to \tau_i)})}{\Gamma \Vdash_x \overline{\kappa_i.\,\tau_i' \to \tau_i} \leadsto (S(\tau_1 \to \tau_2), S)} \ \text{(IMPROVE)}$$

This judgement works as follows. For each equation i of a GADT function x, let $(\kappa_i)_x^\star$ be the set of constraints that mention GADT type constructors (in the constraint set of the type of the i-th equation) and let S_i be the satisfiability substitution for this constraint set, in a typing context that contains type assumptions corresponding to all alternatives. Then, let $\tau_1 \to \tau_2$ be the *lcg* of all $\overline{S_i\,(\tau_i' \to \tau_i)}$. Now, we "skolemize" $\overline{\alpha}$ (i.e. treat them as non-unifiable), the set of type variables introduced by the generalization of types of parameters of a GADT. Type variables that occur in the return type of a function *and* also in the generalization of a parameter of a recursive algebraic type are not skolemized (for example, when the type $[a]$ of the result is obtained from, say, the generalization of $[Int]$ and $[Bool]$). The inferred types of case alternatives are then unified with non-skolemized type variables. The substitutions computed by satisfiability and unification are applied to the generalized type, which is then returned.

It is worth mentioning that the improvement judgement is conservative over non-GADT types, since $\kappa = \emptyset$ when alternative types do not involve GADTs, and no variable is skolemized, so all types must be unified.

3.4 GADT and Principal Type

In [22] Vytiniotis et al. argue that the principal type property offers fewer benefits than a guarantee of type safety (i.e. that well-typed programs will not cause an error at run-time). Consider for example the function *eval*, presented in Sect. 1, but now consider that it is declared with only the first alternative:

$$eval\ (Lit\ i)\ =\ i$$

Our algorithm infers type ($Term\ Int \to Int$) for *eval*, but in Haskell the following type annotations would be allowed for *eval*: $\forall a.\ Term\ a \to a$ and $\forall a.\ Term\ a \to Int$. None of these types is an instance of the other.

In our view, the type $Term\ Int \to Int$ is a good choice in this case, since it avoids expressions such as, for example, *eval* ($IsZ\,(Lit\ 1)$), for which there exists no alternative in the definition of *eval*. With the algorithm given in [22] the following implication constraint is generated during type inference:

$$(a \sim Term\ b) \wedge (b \sim Int \supset c \sim Int)$$

Note that substitution $\{c \mapsto Int\}$ is a solution to this implication constraint and application of this substitution leads to the inference of type $Term\ a \to Int$. However, in this constraint variable c is considered untouchable, and then type inference fails in GHC. Again, in GHC version 7.6.x, the function *eval* defined with only this alternative would have inferred type $\forall a.\ Term\ a \to Int$; from version 7.8.1 type inference fails, due to type variable being considered untouchable.

On the other hand, by adding the alternative of constructor IsZ, where the type $Term\ Bool$ is returned by the constructor, the type of $eval$ becomes: $\forall a.\ Term\ a \to a$, which is the same as the type inferred by our algorithm. It is important to point out that the type $Term\ Int \to Int$, inferred by the alternative of constructor Lit, is an instance of this type, in contrast with the case of $Term\ a \to Int$.

```
eval (Lit i) = i
eval (IsZ i) = 0 == eval i
```

Back to type safety, it would be desirable that in this case the type inference algorithm restricts instances of a to either Int or $Bool$; however, this seems to need a special way of constraining polymorphic types.

In many cases, such as that of Example 1, a relation between the types of alternatives is not expressed by the code in these alternatives. In these cases there is no guarantee that the inferred type is the principal type.

4   Related Work

Peyton Jones *et al.* present an extension of Haskell's type system for the support of GADTs [6,7]. The verification of the types of GADT functions is done using type annotations. These types, called rigid types, are propagated to inner scopes by means of some specific rules. Pottier and Régis-Gianas [12] define a two-pass type inference algorithm, separating traditional Hindley-Milner type inference from the propagation of explicit type annotations. This separation makes the mechanism of type propagation more efficient.

The type inference algorithm used in [15,22], called OutsideIn, extracts type constraints from expressions occurring in inner scopes and solves these constraints in the outermost scope, avoiding an *ad hoc* approach for the propagation of rigid types. Besides using a more natural mechanism for propagation of annotated types, this approach enables more helpful error messages and type inference in a restricted number of function declarations. In these cases a rather restrictive rule is adopted in the definition of untouchable variables, so that only the types of functions for which the existence of a principal type can be guaranteed are inferred. In [19] Sulzmann and Schrijvers introduce some ideas adopted in the OutsideIn algorithm.

Lin and Sheard present the Pointwise GADT type system [9], that uses a modified unification algorithm to support parametric instantiation and type indexing. In [8] Lin proposes algorithm $\mathcal{P}$, more restrictive than Pointwise, that does not require type annotations. The algorithm applies generalization only in patterns of alternatives and supports polymorphic recursion. Differently from our proposal, which handles polymorphic recursion similarly to overloading, algorithm $\mathcal{P}$ uses an approach similar to that used by an iteration limit to guarantee termination.

5   Conclusion

In this paper we have presented a type inference algorithm in the presence of GADTs. The ideas behind the algorithm are intuitive and easy to understand.

The presented algorithm handles alternative definitions of a defined symbol x as if they were overloaded definitions of x, in a closed world approach to overloading, with support for polymorphic recursion. The algorithm makes use of anti-unification to capture the relation between the types of distinct alternatives of a function that has a parameter or returns a GADT. Types which must not be unified are separated, before unifying the types of the alternatives. This enables type inference for functions that typically require type annotations in other implementations, such as that of GHC.

Further study in order to provide support for type annotations is necessary. When there is a relation from the types of arguments to the type of the result of a GADT function which is not made explicit in the code (e.g. Example 3), our type inference algorithm can reject expressions that could be considered type-correct.

References

1. Camarão, C., Figueiredo, L.: Type inference for overloading without restrictions, declarations or annotations. In: Middeldorp, A., Sato, T. (eds.) FLOPS 1999. LNCS, vol. 1722, pp. 37–52. Springer, Heidelberg (1999)
2. Camarão, C., Figueiredo, L., Vasconcellos, C.: Constraint-set Satisfiability for Overloading. In: Proceedings of the 6th ACM SIGPLAN International Conference on Principles and Practice of Declarative Programming, pp. 67–77. ACM (2004)
3. Chang, C.C., Keisler, H.J.: Model Theory: Dover Books on Mathematics, 3rd edn. North-Holland Press, New York (2012)
4. Demoen, B., de la Banda, M.G., Stuckey, P.J.: Type Constraint Solving for Parametric and Ad-hoc Polymorphism. In: Proceedings of the 22nd Australasian Computer Science Conference (1999)
5. Jones, M.: Simplifying and Improving Qualified Types. In: Proceedings of ACM Conference on Functional Programming and Computer Architecture, FPCA 1995, pp. 160–169 (1995)
6. Jones, S.P., Vytiniotis, D., Weirich, S., Washburn, G.: Simple unification-based type inference for GADTs. SIGPLAN Not. **41**(9), 50–61 (2006)
7. Jones, S.P., Washburn, G., Weirich, S.: Wobbly types: type inference for generalised algebraic data types. Technical report MS-CIS-05-26, University of Pennsylvania, Microsoft Research (2004). http://research.microsoft.com/apps/pubs/default.aspx?id=65143
8. Lin, C.K.: Practical type inference for the GADT type system. Ph.D. thesis, Portland State University, Portland, OR, USA (2010)
9. Lin, C.K., Sheard, T.: Pointwise generalized algebraic data types. In: Proceedings of the 5th ACM SIGPLAN Workshop on Types in Language Design and Implementation, TLDI 2010, pp. 51–62. ACM, New York (2010)
10. Plotkin, G.D.: A note on inductive generalisation. Mach. intell. **5**(1), 153–163 (1970)

11. Plotkin, G.D.: A further note on inductive generalisation. Mach. Intell. **6**, 101–124 (1971)
12. Pottier, F., Régis-Gianas, Y.: Stratified type inference for generalized algebraic data types. SIGPLAN Not. **41**(1), 232–244 (2006)
13. Ribeiro, R., Camarão, C.: Ambiguity and context-dependent overloading. J. Braz. Comput. Soc. **19**(3), 313–324 (2013)
14. Ribeiro, R., Camarão, C., Figueiredo, L.: Terminating constraint set satisfiability and simplification algorithms for context-dependent overloading. J. Braz. Comput. Soc. **19**(4), 423–432 (2013)
15. Schrijvers, T., Jones, S.P., Sulzmann, M., Vytiniotis, D.: Complete and decidable type inference for GADTs. SIGPLAN Not. **44**(9), 341–352 (2009)
16. Smith, G.: Polymorphic type inference for languages with overloading and subtyping. Ph.D. thesis, Cornell University (1991)
17. Smith, G.: Principal type schemes for functional programs with overloading and subtyping. Sci. Comput. Program. **23**(2–3), 197–226 (1994)
18. Stuckey, P., Sulzmann, M.: A Theory of overloading. In: Proceedings of the 7th ACM International Conference on Functional Programming, pp. 167–178 (2002)
19. Sulzmann, M., Schrijvers, T., Stuckey, P.J.: Type Inference for GADTs via Herbrand Constraint Abduction (2008)
20. Team, G., et al.: The Glorious Glasgow Haskell Compilation System User's Guide, Version 7.10.1 (2015)
21. Vasconcellos, C.: Inferência de tipos com suporte para sobrecarga baseada no sistema CT. Ph.D. thesis, Universidade Federal de Minas Gerais, Minas Gerais, Brasil (2004)
22. Vytiniotis, D., Jones, S.P., Schrijvers, T., Sulzmann, M.: OutsideIn(X): modular type inference with local assumptions. J. Funct. Program. **21**(4–5), 333–412 (2011)

Preserving Lexical Scoping When Dynamically Embedding Languages

Félix Ribeiro$^{(\boxtimes)}$, Hisham Muhammad, André Murbach Maidl,
and Roberto Ierusalimschy

Department of Computer Science, PUC-Rio, Rio de Janeiro, Brazil
{fribeiro,hisham,amaidl,roberto}@inf.puc-rio.br

Abstract. There are various situations in which one may want to embed source code from one language into another, for example when combining relational query languages with application code or when performing staged meta-programming. Typically, one will want to transfer data between these languages. We propose an approach in which the embedded code shares variables with the host language, preserving lexical scoping rules even after the code is converted into an intermediate representation. We demonstrate this approach through a module for meta programming using Lua as both embedded and host languages. Our technique supports dynamically generated code, requires no special annotation of functions to be translated and is implemented as a library, requiring no source pre-processing or changes to the host language execution environment.

Keywords: Lua · Domain-specific languages · Embedded languages · Meta-programming · Multi-stage programming

1 Introduction

Domain-Specific Languages (DSLs) are a way to simplify the development of programs through the aggregation of domain knowledge into a programming language. A Domain-Specific Language is a programming language that includes features to express the semantics of a domain, often adding specific syntax. Examples of DSLs are TeX for text processing, MATLAB for performing numerical computations, SQL for querying relational databases and regular expressions for pattern matching in text.

The use of DSLs frequently happens in combination with other languages, so that some aspects of a problem are handled with the DSL while other parts are developed in a general-purpose language [7]. One way to do this is to embed source code written in the domain-specific language into the source code of the application, which is written in another language. We have then the notion of a *host language* and an *embedded language*. SQL and regular expressions are examples of languages which are often used in this fashion.

© Springer International Publishing Switzerland 2015
A. Pardo and S.D. Swierstra (Eds.): SBLP 2015, LNCS 9325, pp. 31–43, 2015.
DOI: 10.1007/978-3-319-24012-1_3

Embedding source code of one language into another poses challenges. Typically, a language parser does not have support for handling chunks of code written in another language intermixed with the source code. Common approaches to handle the source code of two languages in a single source file are to either pull the processing back to a step prior to the parsing of the main language, using pre-processing, or to push it forward by storing the code written in the embedded language as strings in the host language source code, which are sent to the embedded language for processing only at run time.

This approach of storing code as strings, while popular, has some inconveniences. For instance, it is not possible to detect syntactical errors while compiling the code. Embedding languages should also allow programmers to transfer data between these languages, taking care to keep data in sync. For these reasons, solutions based on meta-programming, where the embedded language can be manipulated at a higher level of abstraction than strings, are more interesting.

Multi-Stage Programming (MSP) [14–16] is a meta-programming approach that helps embedding a programming language in a host language in a well-organized way. It defines constructs for quoting and escaping source code that produce code objects, which are valid objects stored in the host language but can also be invoked to execute the embedded language. A major benefit of MSP is that it does not delay error verification to run-time. One can detect syntactical errors and even type errors in the embedded code during compile-time. Another benefit of MSP is that we can use program specialization to reduce the costs of abstractions [14].

Using MSP to embed languages inside imperative languages can be hard, because in these languages programmers can move code objects so they are used outside of the scope of the binder of their free variables [17]. In purely functional languages we do not have this problem due to the absence of side effects [9].

Languages that support dynamically-generated code, such as those that provide `eval`-style functions where a string of source code can be compiled into a function object at runtime, present further challenges. Traditional static approaches to meta-programming that work by performing a pre-processing pass at compile time may not be suitable, as the relevant functions may not be generated yet.

In this work, we propose an approach for meta-programming in which the embedded code shares variables with the host language, preserving lexical scoping rules even after the code is converted into an intermediate representation. In our proposed method, the host language uses closures to share data with the embedded language, replacing variable references with function calls in the generated code. This way, we ensure that variables always match the scope of their declarations.

We demonstrate this approach through a module for meta-programming using Lua as both embedded and host languages. Our module decompiles Lua functions to their Abstract Syntax Tree (AST) form and can later rebuild them preserving scoping rules of the decompilation site. For simplicity, our implementation only supports functions that contain a single expression. We call these functions *lambda functions*.

The technique we present here operates entirely at runtime. It is therefore suitable for languages that may be embedded using the dynamic features of the host language.

Our method requires no special annotation of functions to be translated and is implemented as a library, requiring no source pre-processing or changes to the host language execution environment. When an AST describes a function that uses variables from an external local scope, it includes information about the context where this function was defined.

We organize this paper in five sections. In Sect. 2 we review related work in the field of multi-stage programming. In Sect. 3 we demonstrate our approach. In Sect. 4 we formalize the semantics of our approach. In Sect. 5 we present our conclusions.

2   Related Work

Meta-programming is the concept of writing programs that manipulate program code as data, producing other programs. This allows programmers to improve code performance or expressiveness by defining transformations over code. Lisp [11] pioneered meta-programming by introducing a mechanism of *quotation*: expressions marked with the operator ' are not evaluated, and are treated as data. Later Lisp dialects like Common Lisp and Scheme include *quasi-quotation*, represented with the operator ', that allows parts of the quoted expression to be "escaped" (with the , operator). The combination of quasi-quotation and escaping powers the macro system of those languages [1]. This feature, however, does not preserve scoping rules.

Multi-Stage Programming [14–16] is similar to the quasi-quotation mechanism, but it takes lexical scoping into account. It features three constructs that programmers can use to annotate code: *brackets*, *escape*, and *run*. We will use MetaOCaml [2], an OCaml extension with MSP support through these three staging constructs, to briefly explain these constructs. *Brackets*, marked with .<>., avoid the execution of a computation, constructing an object instead that represents the marked block of code:

```
let x = 1 + 1;;
let y = .< 1 + 1 >.;;
```

In the above example, x has type int and y has type int code. This means that the expression x + y is invalid code in MetaOCaml, as the types of both variables do not match. *Escapes*, marked as .~ , combine small delayed computations for building bigger ones:

```
let z = .< x + .~y >.;;
```

Here, the code .< x + .~y >. binds a new delayed computation 2 + (1 + 1) to z. *Run*, using the prefix operator .!, executes staged code. In the example below, the program will compile and execute the code inside z, assigning the integer 4 to r:

```
let r = .!z;;
```

Implementing DSLs is one of the most interesting applications of MSP [3]. Implementing efficient DSLs, either as interpreters or as compilers, is not an easy task. The MSP constructs allow programmers to implement a DSL as a staged interpreter, which translates the DSL code to the host language code, allowing DSLs to run as efficiently as the host code, taking advantage of the optimizations of the underlying compiler [15].

Mint [17] is a MSP extension to Java. Even though MSP ensures correctness while embedding languages using purely functional languages, the same is not that straightforward when we try to use MSP for embedding imperative languages. The problem of embedding a language in an imperative language is related to side effects, as programmers can move code objects beyond the bound scope of free variables inadvertently, a problem known as scope extrusion. Mint extends the semantics of the escape construct to impose some restrictions on side effects, not allowing side effects to appear inside a escape construct when these side effects interact with delayed code.

LINQ (Language Integrated-Query) [12] is a set of features that extends C#, allowing programmers to perform queries and manipulate data over different kinds of data storage such as XML and MDF. One can also use LINQ with data structures such as lists and arrays.

In .NET, C# and Visual Basic define a restricted type of anonymous function called an *expression lambda*, which is a function that consists of a single expression. LINQ works as an embedded DSL [7] where anonymous functions are used extensively, and was the motivating use case for the introduction of expression lambdas. When one assigns an expression lambda to a variable of type `Expression<TDelegate>`, .NET creates an AST corresponding to that expression, called an *expression tree*[1]. Expression trees can also be created programatically, manipulating node objects via the API of the `Expression` class.

Expression lambdas can access external local variables, and they respect lexical scope, regardless if they are used to declare anonymous functions or only to produce an expression tree. Figure 1 illustrates how lexical scoping is preserved in expression trees. Free variable y in line 5 references the declaration from line 4, even when the expression tree returned in line 11 is compiled into a function in line 12.

Terra [4] is a multi-stage language for high-performance computing. It uses Lua as a host language and defines extensions for staged computation. Lua functions that run in the Lua interpreter are declared using standard Lua syntax, with the `function` construct. Staged code is declared as Terra functions, using the `terra` statement. Terra functions use similar syntax to Lua, but they are statically typed and compiled into native code using LLVM. Lua code can manipulate Terra types and functions as Lua objects. Terra also features a `quote`

---

[1] Note that in C# parlance, *lambda expression* is a more general term that can refer to both single-expression anonymous functions called *expression lambdas* and multi-statement functions called *statement lambdas*. Conversion to expression trees is only supported for expression lambdas.

```
1    class Program {
2      delegate int sumY (int arg);
3      Expression <sumY> boo () {
4        int y = 1;
5        Expression <sumY> treesumY = x => x + y;
6        y = y + 1;
7        return treesumY;
8      }
9      int foo () {
10       int y = 10;
11       Expression <sumY> ret = boo();
12       return ret.Compile()(40); // returns 42
13     }
14   }
```

Fig. 1. Lexical scoping in variables referenced in expression trees in C#.

statement for quoting blocks of Terra code as expression objects and brackets ([]) as the escape operator for evaluating Lua code inside a Terra function.

When a Terra function is declared, all Lua expressions escaped inside it and Lua variables are replaced by the results of their evaluation. A Terra function, therefore, does not form a closure with respect to free Lua variables. This design trades lexical scoping for the guarantee that compiled Terra code does not need to call back into the Lua interpreter during execution.

Metalua [5] is a Lua compiler that supports compile-time meta-programming, a mechanism that allows programmers to interact with the compiler through a macro system [6]. Metalua extends Lua 5.1 to provide methods for transforming Lua code into Abstract Syntax Trees, but this code cannot contain references to local variables of an outer scope.

Our implementation generates program ASTs in the same format as Metalua, but including information about enclosing local variables. While Metalua handles arbitrary Lua code syntactically marked for quoting, our module operates only on restricted functions, but requires no quoting.

3   Lua2AST

We now present our proposed approach for run-time meta-programming. We begin by describing in this section our implementation, Lua2AST. In the following section, we proceed by formally discussing its semantics.

Lua2AST is a Lua module that is able to generate ASTs given a restricted form of Lua functions, that we named lambda functions. Lambda functions are defined as functions that contain in its body a single **return** statement containing an expression. This expression can be of any kind and can also use variables of the outer lexical scope.

Lua supports functions as a first-class value. Function objects are proper closures, and are internally implemented by storing along with each function a internal set of boxed references any `local` variables belonging to outer lexical scopes. In Lua, these references are called *upvalues* [8]. Upvalues implement proper lexical scoping and are generally transparent to the Lua programmer, but they can be directly manipulated through Lua's C API and through its debug API. Lua2AST can produce a Lua function object given an AST, and references to variables in the resulting function match the lexical scoping rules of the call site where the AST was originally generated. As we will see below, this is done using the debug API to correct upvalue references in the generated code.

Lua2AST uses two external Lua libraries in its implementation: LuaDec and Lua-Parser. Luadec [13] is a Lua decompiler that takes a Lua binary chunk and returns a string with equivalent Lua source code. Lua-Parser [10] generates a Lua table representing the code AST given a string of Lua source code. Lua2AST works by decompiling the input function with LuaDec, producing an AST with Lua-Parser and finally resolving upvalue references in this AST, producing an annotated AST with additional information that allows the library to recreate the function's original environment.

Our approach to preserve variable references is to generate auxiliary closures when converting the function into AST format. These auxiliary closures are stored in the AST data structure. When compiling the AST back into a function, variable references are replaced by function calls to these closures.

This approach presents two major advantages to usual methods for adding staged computation to existing languages. Firstly, our implementation is done entirely as a library. By internally using a decompiler, we can operate directly on Lua function objects without having to use a source code preprocessor. This results in a non-intrusive approach: we did not need to create language extensions and we did not need to modify the Lua virtual machine.

Secondly, our approach is particularly suitable for a dynamic language. If Lua2AST was implemented as a static pass over the input source code, it would not be possible to transform dynamically-loaded functions into ASTs. Since Lua2AST operates entirely at runtime, we are able to operate over any suitable lambda function, including dynamically-generated Lua functions, such as those loaded during program execution using the `dostring` function.

Below, we will discuss the implementation in further detail, covering the two main functions of the Lua2AST API: `lua2ast.toAST` and `lua2ast.compile`.

3.1   Function Lua2ast.toAST(*func*)

The function `toAST` generates an AST from a Lua function. It takes a Lua function as a parameter, which must be a lambda function. The function's return is a Lua table that represents an AST. This table follows a standardized format for Lua ASTs that was originally defined by the Metalua project [5]. If the received function uses upvalues, this AST will be decorated with additional data, so that upvalue references can be later reconstructed.

The function `toAST` initially calls the LuaDec decompiler to produce a source code representation of the given function. This string is sent to the `parse` function of the Lua-Parser library, producing the AST that represents the code.

The AST as returned by Lua-Parser, however, would not be sufficient to reconstruct the function with proper scoping rules. Simply rebuilding the plain AST
into source code and loading into Lua would produce a function where all local
variables of outer scopes would turn into global variable references, since in Lua
undeclared variables are treated as globals by default.

The next step, therefore, is to detect locals of outer scopes and to annotate
them in the AST. This is done by scanning variable references in the AST and
matching them to the list of upvalues of the function object. Firstly, we find the
parameters of the function and store them in a set. Then, we locate the free
variables of the function, which are indentifiers in our expression tree that are
not in the set of function arguments. These free identifiers may be references to
outer locals or references to global variables. Any outer local will have a matching
entry in the internal list of upvalues of the closure. We look for this entry using
debug.getupvalue(), a function of Lua's standard library that allows us to
perform introspection of a function's upvalues. When the variable is found, we
decorate the AST node.

To do this decoration in our AST, we create a closure which will hold a
reference to our desired variable. To do so, we use the following helper function:

```
local function newclosure()
    local temp
    return function () return temp end
end
```

This function produces a new closure that contains an upvalue and merely
returns it. We then use the function debug.upvaluejoin(), also from the standard library. This function gets an upvalue from a Lua closure and make it
refer to another upvalue from a different function. We take the upvalue from
our desired variable and join it with the upvalue for the temp variable of our
newly-created closure. We then store this auxiliary closure in the AST node
that identifies the free variable.

Figure 2 illustrates the use of the lua2ast.toAST() function. The Lua code
on this example operates equivalently to the code on Fig. 1. For illustration
purposes, the code also calls lua2ast.print(), which dumps the AST in textual
format, following the syntax of Metalua. It represents node types with names
such as 'Function; node data is represented as strings such as "x". The output
produced by the call at line 7 would be as follows:

```
{ 'Function{ { 'Id "x" },
    { 'Return{ 'Op{ "add", 'Id "x", 'Id "y"}}}
}}
```

Node 'Id "y" is internally decorated with a closure that returns the value
of y defined in line 4.

```
1     local lua2ast = require "lua2ast"
2
3     function boo()
4          local y = 1
5          local treesumY = lua2ast.toAST(function(x) return x + y end)
6          y = y + 1
7          lua2ast.print(treesumY)
8          return treesumY
9     end
10
11    function foo()
12         local y = 10
13         local ret = boo()
14         return lua2ast.compile(ret)(40) -- returns 42
15    end
```

Fig. 2. Lua2AST usage example

3.2   Function Lua2ast.compile(*ast*)

This function takes an AST and returns a new function object that is a result of the AST's compilation. When used with ASTs generated by lua2ast.toAST(), it will use the additional decoration to produce variable references with proper lexical scope.

Function lua2ast.toAST() works by generating source code, compiling it and then using the standard debug library's facilities to attach the auxiliary closures to the generated function's upvalue slots.

Proceeding with the example of Fig. 2, the AST returned in line 13 would be initially converted into the following source code (Lua uses double-brackets for multi-line strings):

```
[[ local y
   return function(x) return x + y() end ]]
```

Prior to the reconstructed source code of the functions, we add declarations of local variables for each outer local variable referenced in the function. Note also that references for these variables are replaced by function calls in the body of the function.

We then compile this source code using Lua's standard function loadstring() and run it to obtain its return value: a Lua function object. Note that in the value of local y is not assigned in the source code. Calling this function at this point would result in an error as the upvalue for y points to a variable with the value of nil.

The final step of lua2ast.compile() is to fix the upvalue references to make them point to the auxiliary closures created by lua2ast.toAST() and stored in the AST table. For that, we use the standard function debug.setupvalue(), which takes a closure, an upvalue index and a Lua value, and sets the variable

$$e = b \,|\, x \,|\, \text{let } x = e \text{ in } e \,|\, x := e \,|\, e(e) \,|\, \text{fun}(x)\{e\} \,|\, e \text{ op } e \,|\, \text{toAST}(e) \,|\, \text{compile}(a)$$
$$v = b \,|\, \langle \Gamma, x, e \rangle \,|\, a$$
$$a = [\text{fn } x \ a] \,|\, [\text{base } b] \,|\, [\text{var } x \ \langle \Gamma, x, e \rangle] \,|\, [\text{op } a \ a]$$

Fig. 3. Syntax of our version of Lua Core, extended with constructs to specify Lua2AST

pointed by the upvalue to the given value. It is worth pointing out, however, that by setting this value we are not fixing the value of the original variable reference (y from line 5 in Fig. 2). This reference was replaced in the newly generated function with a call to a proxy function (y() in the above example), and it is this new local y variable which is having its value fixed with the correct proxy function instead. We formalize this process precisely in the following section.

Once the upvalues are fixed, lua2ast.compile() returns the function. In line 14 of Fig. 2 we see that the result of the compilation is then further applied, and the reconstructed function runs according to the scope of the original function declared in line 5.

4   Semantics

In this section, we specify the behavior of functions lua2ast.toAST() and lua2ast.compile() by using the formalization of a subset of Lua semantics, presented in [4] as Lua Core. We use the same formal framework of that work in order to properly compare and contrast our approach for multi-stage programming to that employed by Terra.

Lua Core depicts the notions of lexical scoping, closures and side-effects present in Lua, and is therefore mostly sufficient for our purposes. We extend this specification with an arbitrary "binary operator" expression, mimicking Lua operators supported by Lua2AST. This way, we have a recursive rule through which we can model Lua expressions as trees, to be later converted to ASTs. We also include $toAST()$ and $compile()$ as core language operations so we can specify their semantics separately from plain functions.

The syntax of our version of Lua Core is presented in Fig. 3. A Lua expression (e) can be either a base value (b), a variable (x), a scoped variable definition (let $x = e$ in e, with $e_1; e_2$ as sugar for let_ $= e_1$ in e_2), a variable assignment ($x := e$), an application ($e(e)$), a function definition (fun(x)\{e\}), an operation on expressions (e op e), or one of the special invocations $toAST(e)$ and $compile(a)$. Lua values (v) can be base values (b), Lua ASTs (a) or closures. A closure is represented as a triple $\langle \Gamma, x, e \rangle$, consisting of a namespace $\Gamma : x \to p$ (mapping variable names x to memory positions p), an input argument x and an expression body e. A Lua AST for a function consists of a root node ([fn $x\ a$]) which may contain nodes that wrap base values ([base b]), operations ([op $a\ a$]), and variables ([var $x\ \langle \Gamma, x, e \rangle$]). As we will see below, the fact that variables are wrapped by a node containing a closure is central to our approach.

In Fig. 4, we present the rules for evaluating Lua Core over an environment Σ, which is a tuple (Γ, S) containing a namespace $\Gamma : x \to p$ and a store

$$v, \Sigma \xrightarrow{L} v, \Sigma \;\; (\text{LVal}) \qquad\qquad b, \Sigma \xrightarrow{D} [\text{base } b] \;\; (\text{DBase})$$

$$\frac{\Sigma = (\Gamma, S)}{x, \Sigma \xrightarrow{L} S(\Gamma(x)), \Sigma} \;\; (\text{LVar}) \qquad\qquad \frac{\Sigma = (\Gamma, S)}{x, \Sigma \xrightarrow{D} [\text{var } x \; \langle \Gamma, \_, x \rangle]} \;\; (\text{DVar})$$

$$\frac{\begin{array}{c} e_1, \Sigma_1 \xrightarrow{L} v_1, (\Gamma_2, S_2) \quad p \, \text{fresh} \\ e_2, (\Gamma_2[x \leftarrow p], S_2[p \leftarrow v_1]) \xrightarrow{L} v_2, (\Gamma_3, S_3) \end{array}}{\text{let } x = e_1 \; \text{in} \, e_2, \Sigma_1 \xrightarrow{L} v_2, (\Gamma_2, S_3)} \;\; (\text{LLet}) \qquad \frac{e_1, \Sigma \xrightarrow{D} a_1 \quad e_2, \Sigma \xrightarrow{D} a_2}{e_1 \text{ op } e_2, \Sigma \xrightarrow{D} [\text{op } a_1 \, a_2]} \;\; (\text{DOp})$$

$$\frac{\begin{array}{c} e_1, \Sigma_1 \xrightarrow{L} \langle \Gamma_1, x, e_3 \rangle, \Sigma_2 \\ e_2, \Sigma_2 \xrightarrow{L} v_1, (\Gamma_3, S_3) \quad p \, \text{fresh} \\ e_3, (\Gamma_1[x \leftarrow p], S_3[p \leftarrow v_1]) \xrightarrow{L} v_2, (\Gamma_4, S_4) \end{array}}{e_1(e_2), \Sigma_1 \xrightarrow{L} v_2, (\Gamma_3, S_4)} \;\; (\text{LApp}) \qquad \frac{e, \Sigma \xrightarrow{D} a}{\langle \Gamma, x, e \rangle, \Sigma \xrightarrow{D} [\text{fn } x \, a]} \;\; (\text{DFn})$$

$$[\text{base } b], \Sigma \xrightarrow{C} b, \Sigma \;\; (\text{CBase})$$

$$\frac{e_1, \Sigma_1 \xrightarrow{L} v, (\Gamma, S) \quad \Gamma(x) = p}{x := e, \Sigma \xrightarrow{L} v, (\Gamma, S[p \leftarrow v])} \;\; (\text{LAsn})$$

$$\frac{\Sigma = (\Gamma, S)}{\text{fun}(x)\{e\}, \Sigma \xrightarrow{L} \langle \Gamma, x, e \rangle, \Sigma} \;\; (\text{LFun}) \qquad \frac{\begin{array}{c} \Sigma_1 = (\Gamma, S) \\ p \, \text{fresh} \\ \Sigma_2 = (\Gamma[x \leftarrow p], S[p \leftarrow f]) \end{array}}{[\text{var } x \; f], \Sigma_1 \xrightarrow{C} x(\_), \Sigma_2} \;\; (\text{CVar})$$

$$\frac{\begin{array}{c} e_1, \Sigma_1 \xrightarrow{L} v_1, \Sigma_2 \quad e_2, \Sigma_2 \xrightarrow{L} v_2, \Sigma_3 \\ v_3 = Op(v_1, v_2) \end{array}}{e_1 \text{ op} \, e_2, \Sigma_1 \xrightarrow{L} v_3, \Sigma_3} \;\; (\text{LOp}) \qquad \frac{a_1, \Sigma_1 \xrightarrow{C} e_1, \Sigma_2 \quad a_2, \Sigma_2 \xrightarrow{C} e_2, \Sigma_3}{[\text{op } a_1 \, a_2], \Sigma_1 \xrightarrow{C} e_1 \text{ op } e_2, \Sigma_3} \;\; (\text{COp})$$

$$\frac{e_1, \Sigma_1 \xrightarrow{L} \langle \Gamma, x, e_2 \rangle, \Sigma_2 \quad \langle \Gamma, x, e_2 \rangle, \Sigma_2 \xrightarrow{D} a}{\text{toAST}(e_1), \Sigma_1 \xrightarrow{L} a, \Sigma_2} \;\; (\text{LAst}) \qquad \frac{\begin{array}{c} \Sigma_1 = (\Gamma_1, S_1) \\ a, \Sigma_1 \xrightarrow{C} e, (\Gamma_2, S_2) \end{array}}{[\text{fn } x \, a], \Sigma_1 \xrightarrow{C} \langle \Gamma_2, x, e \rangle, (\Gamma_1, S_2)} \;\; (\text{CFn})$$

$$\frac{a, \Sigma_1 \xrightarrow{C} e, \Sigma_2 \quad e \xrightarrow{L} v}{\text{compile}(a), \Sigma_1 \xrightarrow{L} v, \Sigma_2} \;\; (\text{LComp})$$

Fig. 4. Rules $\xrightarrow{L}$ for the evaluation of Lua expressions, $\xrightarrow{D}$ for decompiling Lua expressions into ASTs, and $\xrightarrow{C}$ for compiling ASTs back into expressions.

$S : p \to v$ that maps memory positions to values[2]. We use $\xrightarrow{L} : (e \times \Sigma) \to (v \times \Sigma)$ for the evaluation of Lua expressions as in [4]. Rules for $\xrightarrow{L}$ presented here are equivalent to those in that work: LVal and LVar evaluate values and variables; LLet describes variable scoping, by evaluating e_2 in an environment created by adding the result of evaluating e_1 and assigning it to local variable x; LApp describes function application, propagating side effects; LAsn evaluates assignments; LFun evaluates function declarations. Our work adds new rules

---

[2] The semantics of Lua Core in [4] is based on an environment $\Sigma = (\Gamma, S, F)$ where F is specific to Terra functions. In our presentation, we removed F. Rules reused from [4] were adapted accordingly.

for $\xrightarrow{L}$: LOP describes the evaluation of an arbitrary binary operator, with semantics given by some function $Op()$; LAST describes the evaluation of $toAST()$; LCOMP evaluates $compile()$.

We also add two other relations: rules for decompiling a Lua function into an AST $(\xrightarrow{D}: (e \times \Sigma) \to a)$ and rules for compiling ASTs back into Lua functions $(\xrightarrow{C}: (a \times \Sigma) \to (e \times \Sigma))$. These are used in LAST and LCOMP, respectively.

The decompilation function $\xrightarrow{D}$ takes an expression and an environment and produces an AST. Since $toAST()$ is a pure function, Σ does not figure in the codomain of $\xrightarrow{D}$. Note that $\xrightarrow{D}$ is defined only for base values (DBASE), variables (DVAR), the binary operator (DOP), and the initial function (DFN), mirroring the implementation of $toAST()$ in Lua2AST, which only supports functions containing these elements. Its rules deconstruct the body of the function and build the corresponding AST. Of particular interest is rule DVAR, which stores in the AST node a newly created closure, which returns the value of x given the original function's environment.

The compilation function $\xrightarrow{C}$ takes an AST and an environment and produces a closure and a new environment. For each of the four decompilation rules there is a complementary compilation rule: CBASE, CVAR, COP and CFN. Rule CVAR translates nodes representing variable references into a function call to the closure created by rule DVAR. CVAR assigns this closure to a variable x in the resulting environment, and produces a function call to this closure instead of a variable reference. Rule CFN returns a closure representing the entire compiled function and a new environment. This environment contains an unmodified namespace Γ_1 and a new store S_2, which includes any closures created for keeping variable references. The extended namespace Γ_2 produced by the compilation is used as the namespace of the resulting function's closure.

As a result of running $compile()$, all variable references that existed in the original function that was decompiled and was now recompiled were replaced by calls to newly-created closures that merely return the value of the corresponding variables. These closures use the original namespace from decompilation time (Γ in DVAR), so the variable references are bound to the addresses they have in the lexical scope where decompilation takes place. Any variable x stored in an AST will only be evaluated when the compiled function returned by $compile(a)$ is called.

By replacing variable references to function calls to the wrapper closures, we ensure that the evaluation of variables (ultimately happening within the wrapper closures) are based on their original namespaces. This is different from the approach taken by Terra [4], where evaluation of Lua variables is done when the Terra code is generated. LINQ [12] preserves the lexical scoping of reconstructed function objects like our work does, but in our case staging happens entirely at run time.

5   Conclusion

In this work we presented an approach for multi-stage programming, through which the lexical scope of variables can be preserved by replacing variable references in the generated representation of the embedded language with closures

42   F. Ribeiro et al.

from the host language. When the intermediate representation is later converted into executable form, calls to these closures are produced, ensuring access to the variable in the correct context.

We implemented a module that demonstrates this approach. Our implementation uses a decompiler to convert, at runtime, Lua functions into an abstract syntax tree form decorated with closures that capture the lexical environment of free variables. The module is then able to compile the AST back into Lua, ensuring that the resulting function accesses the correct variables even if compiled at a different call site.

The technique we present here is general, and its core principle is not dependent on specificities of Lua. It could be implemented in other languages using other methods, such as source code pre-processing. However, the run-time manipulation of function objects made possible by decompilation, as opposed to compile-time manipulation of the source tree, allows us to perform multi-stage programming dynamically, operating on any suitable functions, even if they were created via dynamic code generation. This makes our approach particularly suitable for dynamic languages.

Our implementation also exploited Lua's facilities for manipulating a closure's list of upvalues, which allowed the construction of the generated functions purely through manipulation of Lua function objects, without having to resort to low-level bytecode generation. The only bytecode-level manipulation performed by Lua2AST is read-only, and is restricted to the decompiler module. Our implementation required no language extensions and no modifications to the Lua VM.

We also specified the operational semantics for the transformations performed by Lua2AST, in order to show how the lexical environment of variables is correctly preserved, and to contrast it with related work from the literature on multi-stage programming.

This work presents many possibilities for future extensions. The current implementation is a proof-of-concept that demonstrates the technique, and can be extended to support more of the host language's grammar. Another future work we envision is the development of different code-generation back-ends, supporting other languages. This would allow, for example, using Lua functions for writing prepared statements for database query languages.

References

1. Bawden, A.: Quasiquotation in Lisp. In: Danvy, O. (ed.) Proceedings of the ACM SIGPLAN Workshop on Partial Evaluation and Semantics-Based Program Manipulation (PEPM 1999). Number NS-99-1 in BRICS Note Series, pp. 4–12, San Antonio, Texas (1999)
2. Calcagno, C., Taha, W., Huang, L., Leroy, X.: Implementing multi-stage languages using ASTs, gensym, and reflection. In: Pfenning, F., Macko, M. (eds.) GPCE 2003. LNCS, vol. 2830, pp. 57–76. Springer, Heidelberg (2003)
3. Czarnecki, K., O'Donnell, J.T., Striegnitz, J., Taha, W.: DSL implementation in MetaOCaml, template haskell, and C++. In: Lengauer, C., Batory, D., Blum, A., Odersky, M. (eds.) Domain-Specific Program Generation. LNCS, vol. 3016, pp. 51–72. Springer, Heidelberg (2004)

 4. DeVito, Z., Hegarty, J., Aiken, A., Hanrahan, P., Vitek, J.: Terra: a multi-stage language for high-performance computing. In: Proceedings of the 34th ACM SIG-PLAN Conference on Programming Language Design and Implementation, PLDI 2013, pp. 105–116, New York, NY, USA, ACM (2013)
 5. Fleutot, F.: Metalua: static meta-programming for Lua. https://github.com/fab13n/metalua (2007). Accessed February 2015
 6. Fleutot, F., Tratt, L.: Contrasting compile-time meta-programming in Metalua and converge. In: Proceedings of the Workshop on Dynamic Languages and Applications (2007)
 7. Fowler, M.: Domain Specific Languages, 1st edn. Addison-Wesley Professional, Boston (2010)
 8. Ierusalimschy, R.: Programming in Lua, 2nd edn. Lua.Org (2006)
 9. Kameyama, Y., Kiselyov, O., Shan, C.C.: Closing the stage: from staged code to typed closures. In: Proceedings of the 2008 ACM SIGPLAN Symposium on Partial Evaluation and Semantics-based Program Manipulation, PEPM 2008, pp. 147–157, New York, NY, USA, ACM (2008)
10. Maidl, A.M.: Lua-parser: a Lua 5.3 parser written with LPeg. https://github.com/andremm/lua-parser (2013). Accessed April 2015
11. McCarthy, J.: Recursive functions of symbolic expressions and their computation by machine, part I. Commun. ACM **3**(4), 184–195 (1960)
12. Microsoft: LINQ.   https://msdn.microsoft.com/en-us/library/bb397926.aspx (2013). Accessed April 2015
13. Muhammad, H.: LuaDec: a decompiler for the Lua language. http://luadec.luaforge.net/ (2006). Accessed April 2015
14. Taha, W.: Multi-stage programming: its theory and applications. Ph.D thesis, Oregon Graduate Institute of Science and Technology (1999)
15. Taha, W.: A gentle introduction to multi-stage programming. In: Lengauer, C., Batory, D., Blum, A., Odersky, M. (eds.) Domain-Specific Program Generation. LNCS, vol. 3016, pp. 30–50. Springer, Heidelberg (2004)
16. Taha, W.: A gentle introduction to multi-stage programming, part II. In: Lämmel, R., Visser, J., Saraiva, J. (eds.) Generative and Transformational Techniques in Software Engineering II. LNCS, vol. 5235, pp. 260–290. Springer, Heidelberg (2008)
17. Westbrook, E., Ricken, M., Inoue, J., Yao, Y., Abdelatif, T., Taha, W.: Mint: java multi-stage programming using weak separability. In: Proceedings of the 2010 ACM SIGPLAN Conference on Programming Language Design and Implementation, PLDI 2010, pp. 400–411, New York, NY, USA, ACM (2010)

The Dinamica Virtual Machine for Geosciences

Bruno Morais Ferreira, Britaldo Silveira Soares-Filho,
and Fernando Magno Quintão Pereira[(✉)]

UFMG, Avenida Antônio Carlos, 6627, Belo Horizonte 31270-010, Brazil
{brunomf,fernando}@dcc.ufmg.br, britaldo@csr.ufmg.br

Abstract. This paper describes DinamicaVM, the virtual machine that
runs applications developed in Dinamica EGO. Dinamica EGO is a
framework used in the development of geomodeling applications. Behind
its multitude of visual modes and graphic elements, Dinamica EGO runs
on top of a virtual machine. This machine - DinamicaVM - offers developers a rich instruction set architecture, featuring elements such as map
and reduce, which are typical in the functional/parallel world. Ensuring
that these very expressive components work together efficiently is a challenging endeavour. Dinamica's runtime addresses this challenge through
a suite of optimizations, which borrows ideas from functional programming languages, and leverages specific behavior expected in geo-scientific
programs. As we show in this paper some of these optimizations deliver
speedups of almost 50x, and are key to the industrial-quality performance
of one of the world's most widely used geomodeling tools.

1 Introduction

Dinamica EGO is a framework that supports the development of geomodeling
applications [17]. It was first released in 1998, and since then it has grown to
enjoy international recognition as an effective and useful framework for geomodeling. It has been used to model carbon emission and deforestation [13], biodiversity loss [15], urbanization and climate change [11], emission reduction [9]
and urban growth [19]. Testimony of Dinamica's maturity are the intergovern-
mental collaborations where it is used. Among its application to public policies
in collaboration with governmental institutions in Brazil and abroad we cite the
World Bank and the United Nations Development Programme. For instance,
the REDD project, which integrates state departments from Bolivia, Peru and
Brazil, is using Dinamica to map the southwestern Amazon[1]. As another example of relevant use, Dinamica's simulation of the environmental impact of the
Santarém-Cuiabá Interstate (BR 163) has been key to lead the Brazilian gov-
ernment to create a national preservation area along this highway[2]. Finally,
SimAmazonia, a large effort to model climate change in the Amazon Basin using
Dinamica EGO [16], is part of the *IPCC*[3] that shared the Nobel Peace prize of
2007 with Al Gore.

---

[1] http://csr.ufmg.br/map/.
[2] http://www.csr.ufmg.br/dinamica/applications/cuiaba-santarem.html.
[3] www.ipcc.ch/publications_and_data/ar4/wg3/en/ch9.html.

© Springer International Publishing Switzerland 2015
A. Pardo and S.D. Swierstra (Eds.): SBLP 2015, LNCS 9325, pp. 44–58, 2015.
DOI: 10.1007/978-3-319-24012-1_4

Dinamica EGO was created as an assemblage of components implemented in C++, called *functors*, which represent typical *cartographic operations* [20]. Each functor has a number of inputs, and produces a number of outputs. The edges that interconnect these ports determine how data flows in a Dinamica's application. The original Dinamica's design had one fundamental disadvantage: functors were complex components implementing complete algorithms. Given this coarse granularity, whenever Dinamica's users needed to implement new behaviors, they had to ask the developers of that framework to code new functors.

To circumvent this shortcoming, we have implemented DinamicaVM, a virtual machine designed to make the Dinamica framework more flexible. The goal of this paper is to describe this virtual machine and its companion programming environment. DinamicaVM contains an instruction set, a library of external components, a scheduler, a garbage collector and an optimizer. The instruction set is built around four functors: *map*, Reduce, Window and While, plus functors for simple operations such as And, Add, Mul, etc. *Map* and Reduce are typical functional-oriented patterns, today heavily used in parallel programming [3]. Henceforth, to avoid confusion with the maps used as Dinamica's main data type, we shall call the *map* functor Apply. Window returns a neighbourhood within a map. While receives a map, and a state, and return a new state which is a function of the input map. In Sect. 3 we introduce, informally, the semantics of each of these four core building-blocks of Dinamica EGO. The architecture that these four components define finds no equal in other systems built with similar purpose, as we explain in Sect. 5.

Applications built in DinamicaEGO manipulate large data: maps having $70\,K \times 70\,K$ cells are common [18]. However, Dinamica's programming environment has been designed with focus on expressivity, not efficiency. *EGO Script*, the graphical programming language that embodies this environment, ensures referential transparency; hence, fostering a functional – side effect free – user experience. In order to ensure that such abstractions can be implemented efficiently, Dinamica applies a number of optimizations onto chains of functors, after these elements are linked together, but before they are deployed in the runtime system. In Sect. 4 we describe these optimizations. Some of these techniques are not new: they have already being implemented in functional languages [21]. Nevertheless, we revisit them under the light of a virtual machine customized to handle maps and tables that represent geographic entities. For instance, even though cache optimizations are well studied, we claim the cache-related transformations from Sect. 4.2 as original contributions of this paper.

2 Dinamica in One Example

We illustrate the basic elements of Dinamica EGO via the implementation of Conway's Game of Life [7]. Figure 1 shows a screenshot of this implementation. The game happens on a two-dimensional grid of square cells. Each cell can be either active or inactive. The state of all the cells in a grid determine a *generation* of the game. Generation $g + 1$ is a function of generation g. The state of cell i at generation $g+1$ is determined by the state of this cell's neighbours, at generation g. The neighbourhood of a cell i is the 3×3 grid centered at i, excluding i itself. If this neighbourhood contains 2 or 3 active cells, i will be active in the next generation, otherwise, it will be inactive. Conway's Game of life is the canonical example of cellular automaton. Dinamica uses, among other techniques, different cellular automata to model land evolution due to human occupation [17].

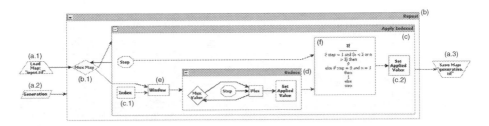

Fig. 1. The implementation of Conway's Game of Life in Dinamica EGO. Letters in parentheses are not part of the original screenshot.

The application in Fig. 1 reads two inputs: an original map (a.1), plus an integer indicating how many generations of the game will be produced (a.2). Its output is the map after the final generation (a.3). A Repeat functor (b) produces the successive generations of the game. Repeat is a specialization of a more general functor called While, which we describe in Sect. 3. Repeat may either read a new map, or work on data that it sends back to its input port. This feedbacking is implemented by a functor called Multiplexer (b.1). Multiplexers are equivalent to the ϕ-functions so ubiquitous in compiler analyses and optimizations [2]. We use an Apply functor (c) to produce generation $g+1$ of the game, given generation g. This component applies some operation on each cell of the input map according to an iterating index (c.1). In this particular example, we are using each Apply's index i to derive a Window (e) of 3×3 cells centered at i. A Reduce operator sums up the number of active cells on each neighbourhood. If this neighbourhood contains 2 or 3 active cells, then i will be active in the next generation, otherwise it will be inactive.

Some of the functors used in this example deal with data-structures. For instance, Window reads a map, plus an index, and returns a neighbourhood within the map. Other functors operate on individual data. For instance, the if container (f) implements a conditional expression made of several smaller components, which we have not shown for the sake of readability. These components, e.g., Equal, And, Or and LessThan, implement unary and binary operations. Users program applications in Dinamica EGO by combining these operators. In particular, the control flow of a Dinamica EGO program is determined by how the different instances of Apply, Reduce, Window and While are interconnected. The next section provides more details about each of these components.

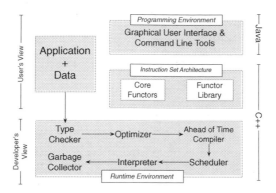

Fig. 2. A schematic view of DinamicaVM.

3   The Dinamica Virtual Machine

Dinamica EGO runs on a virtual machine called DinamicaVM. Figure 2 shows a schematic view of this virtual machine, including its programming environment. Dinamica provides its users with a Graphical User Interface, which is implemented in Java. It is also possible to load and run applications via a suite of command line tools. These applications are ensembles of functors. This virtual machine uses a set of functors, which include Apply, Reduce, While and Window. It also provides a library of components, which exist either due to efficiency reasons, or to keep compatibility with applications built prior to Dinamica 2.4.

The runtime environment of Dinamica EGO consists of an optimizer, and ahead-of-time compiler, a scheduler, an interpreter and a garbage collector. The ahead-of-time compiler converts Apply expressions, i.e., expressions that will be applied on every cell of a map or table, into binary code. These expressions are defined by Dinamica's user through a syntax that we call *EGO Script*. Translation to binary works in two steps: first EGO Script commands are converted to C++ instructions. Then, these instructions are compiled into binary code by gcc. The scheduler sorts the functors topologically, and forwards this information to the interpreter. If the target machine has multiple cores, then the scheduler parallelizes the execution of functors according to their dependences. The memory occupied by data structures that are no longer used are reclaimed by a garbage collector, which is based on reference counting. Cyclic dependences are not a problem in Dinamica, as it is not possible to create circular structures in it. In this section, we shall explore the four key components that this virtual machine interprets: Apply, Reduce, Window and While.

Apply. The Apply functor receives two inputs: (i) a map m, whose each cell has type t, e.g., $m : Map\langle t \rangle$, and (ii) a function $f : t \mapsto t$, that transforms the contents of each cell. The functor then applies f onto each cell of m, yielding a new map m'. Figure 3(a) provides a visual representation of Apply when used in a program that increments every cell of a matrix of integers. The shapes used

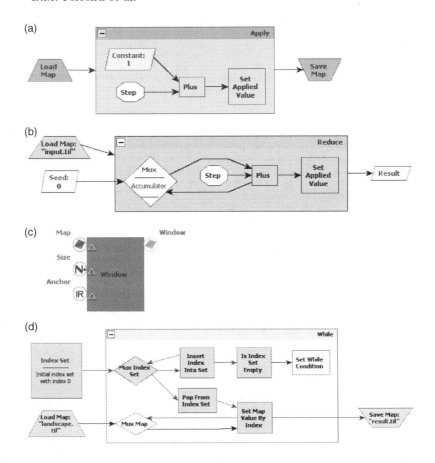

Fig. 3. The four high-level functors in DinamicaVM's instruction set architecture. (a) Apply; (b) Reduce; (c) Window; (d) While.

here are pragmatic. They are just visual triggers to help the user to identify the functors and its ports.

In Dinamica's Jargon, Apply is a Container. A Container is a functor that may incorporate other functors. In terms of implementation, Containers follow the "composite" design pattern [6]. Containers, like every other functor, may have input and output ports. An Apply has only one input port, which receives the target map, and only one output port, which yields the new version of the map. However, contrary to regular functors, Containers have also *internal* ports, which are used to communicate with their components. Apply has only two internal ports. The first is Step, which returns the contents of a cell of the input map. This element keeps an internal state, in such a way that successive invocations of it return always different elements, which come from contiguous positions in a column-major traversal of the map. The second internal port is Set, which causes a value to be written in a position of the output map that corresponds to the last index visited by Step in the input map.

Apply is one of the most used components in the Dinamica's ecosystem. Examples of its use include mapping coordinates into administrative regions such as countries, states and municipalities; mapping altitude into costs; mapping cells into slope values, which are calculated given these cells's neighbours, etc. Thus, it is very important that this component be implemented efficiently. Each iteration of Apply uses data that is completely independent from the data used by the other iterations. In the PRAM (*parallel random-access machine*) model, Apply can be implemented to run in $O(1)$. Thus, this functor is implemented to run in parallel.

Reduce. Reduce takes a map m of type $Map\langle t\rangle$, a binary operator $\oplus$, of type $t' \times t \mapsto t'$, and a seed s of type t'. It then produces a single value v of type t', such that $v = s \oplus m[0] \oplus m[1] \oplus \ldots \oplus m[n-1]$. In this case, $m[0], \ldots m[n-1]$ are all the cells in m, assuming that m has n cells. Figure 3(b) shows an application that sums up all the elements in a map of integers, thus producing an integer as its result.

Like Apply, Reduce is also a Container. It has one internal input, Set, which bears the same semantics as the component of same name in Apply. It has one internal output port, Step, which delivers to the internal functors the current value of the iteration. A functor Mux performs the function of the accumulator used to keep track of the current value of a reduction. This functor, if applied on a $n_1 \times n_2$ map, runs sequentially in $O(n_1 \times n_2)$. We can parallelize it for a few operations, which are commutative and associative, such as summation, multiplication, minimum and maximum. In this case, it runs in $O(\ln(n_1 \times n_2))$ in the PRAM model.

Window. Several applications implemented in Dinamica use small neighbourhoods within a map: finding the average slope of a coordinate, with regard to its neighbours; detecting borders, smoothing images, applying convolutions, finding minimum/maximal cost paths, etc. Therefore, Dinamica provides users with an operator to find neighbourhoods in maps: the Window functor, whose inputs and output are represented in Fig. 3(c).

Window has three inputs ports, which receive a map, the size of a neighbourhood's side and an anchor, e.g., the coordinate that is the center of the neighbourhood. It outputs a set of cells that constitute the neighbourhood. The vast majority of all the algorithms built in Dinamica use squared neighbourhoods whose sides contain an odd number of elements, and whose center point is the anchor. Because this setup is so common, it is heavily optimized, as we explain in Sect. 4.2.

While. Most of Dinamica EGO components are stateless. Data structures are usually copies, instead of being modified in place, for instance. However, there are cases when keeping track of state is desirable for efficiency reason. For instance, a stateless functor to model the movement of a ball, under the force of gravity only, when let loose onto an elevation map, could lead to a formidable number of copies of the target map. Dinamica avoids such situations by providing users with a statefull functor – the While iterator. The graphical representation of this element can be seen in Fig. 3(d).

An While has one input port, which receives an *index set*. An index set is a collection of sortable elements that index a data-structure: coordinates on a 2D or 3D map, points on a line, rows in a table, etc. The While has an internal Step port, which keeps track of the elements in the index set still to be processed. While also has an internal Set port, which may update the index set with new elements. Thus, in practice, While implements worklists: as long as the worklist is not empty, this functor perform an action. DinamicaVM uses While, for instance, to implement searches by depth and breadth in maps. A very common index set consists in contiguous sequences of integer numbers. This case is so common that we have a specialization of While – the Repeat functor – optimized to use it.

Specific Components. The While functor seen in Sect. 3, plus the binary and unary operators of Dinamica EGO define a Turing complete language. Turing completeness comes from the fact that these functors subsume the **While** formalism, typically used to illustrate programming language semantics [14]. Nevertheless, there are applications that do not translate easily into amalgamations of these few elements. In particular, there exist behaviors that our optimizations from Sect. 4 do not derive automatically. Thus, Dinamica EGO provides a few specific – higher-level – components which are not implemented as combinations of the four previously described functors. These components are also necessary to keep compatibility with applications developed prior to Dinamica v2.4, which did not use the virtual machine that we describe in this paper. This library includes a set of small functors with utilities purpose. This functors are for arithmetical operations and helpers for loops (such as muxes).

For instance, Dinamica EGO contains a functor called CalcCostMap, which constructs cost-surface maps out of raster images [4]. This functor has two inputs: a friction map, and a map of source points. The outcome of a cost calculation is a map that tells us, for each cell, the minimum cost to reach one of the source cells. This problem emerges, for instance, whenever it is necessary to determine the paths that roads must traverse to link each interior city to a given set of harbours. The cost calculation problem is usually solved via chaotic iterations. We start with a solution map in which each cell is mapped to an infinitely large cost. Then, we iterate successive applications of the operator below, until a fixed point is reached:

$$cost(x) = min \begin{cases} cost(x) \\ cost(y) + friction(x) \\ sqrt(2) \times (cost(z) + friction(x)) \end{cases}$$

z	y	z
y	x	y
z	y	z

We have implemented the chaotic iterations as successive applications of four loops, whose iteration space is given in Fig. 4(a). Each of these loops is parallelized independently. Figure 4(b) shows the pattern of dependences in the first loop, which traverses the map from the upper-left corner towards the lower-right corner. The execution runtime has a predefined number of available workers. Each worker has a task queue and can run a single task at a time. Tiles that

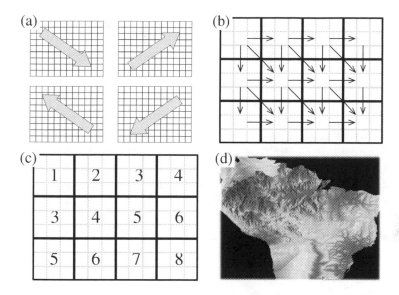

Fig. 4. (a) The four loops that implement the chaotic iterations of the CalcCostMap functor. (b) Dependencies between tiles in the first loop: upper-left to lower-right. (c) Tiles with the same number can be processed together in the first loop. (d) Example of cost map that Dinamica produces.

must be processed are organized as a digraph of pending tasks. Tasks become eligible to run after all their dependencies have been processed. If a thread is idle, then it reclaims a tile that has no pending dependencies. This pattern continues until all the tiles have been processed. If the task queue of a processor becomes empty, then it might steal work from the queue of other processor. If a thread cannot steal any task, then it votes for the end of the computation. The computation terminates when a consensus is achieved among all the workers.

In the previous Dinamica EGO architecture, the granularity of composition was much higher. That is to say that users make use of fewer components to build applications, but these components themselves, were already fairly complex, implementing very specific algorithms themselves. Optimizations were only inside functors or very specific [5]. Now, we have programmable blocks that can be combined in a much finer granularity. It enables the implementation of more general optimizations as we describe next.

4   Optimizations

In order to be accepted by its users, the Dinamica Virtual Machine had to be at least as efficient as the original implementation of Dinamica's runtime, which was used until Dinamica v2.4, last released in 2014. The key to achieve this efficiency are optimizations. Not only the implementations of Apply, Reduce, While and Window are highly engineered, but also the way that these components interact is optimized. All the optimizations that we describe here, except the prefetching from Sect. 4.2[4], are applied after an application has been type checked, but before its modules start to run. EGO Script's type system is static, i.e., types are known before an application starts running. Furthermore, this language does not support the dynamic loading of components, like PHP or JavaScript do. Therefore, we know the size of each map cell that is manipulated within an application, and we have a complete view of the dependence graph between components. This knowledge is important to generate code for the routines that read data, and move data between different functors. In this section we briefly touch the most important transformations that DinamicaVM applies onto its building blocks before an application runs. All the numbers that we show alongside the description of the optimization have been obtained in an Intel Core i5 with clock of 2.67GHz and 8GB of RAM.

4.1 Fusion

Fusion is a transformation that we implement onto combinations of Apply + Apply, and Apply + Reduce. This optimization is common in functional languages [21]. It consists in combining the operators used by different functors in the following way:

$$\text{Apply } f \ (\text{Apply } g \ m) = \text{Apply } (f \circ g) \ m$$

$$\text{Reduce } s \ f \ (\text{Apply } g \ m) = \text{Reduce } s \ f' \ m$$
$$\text{where } f = \lambda(x, y) \ . \ x \oplus y$$
$$\text{and } f' = \lambda(x, y) \ . \ g(x) \oplus y$$

Function fusion is not a new idea of ours. If fact, we are using a very limited form of fusion, as we only apply it to two combinations of functions. More extensive implementations have been described, for instance, by Jones *et al.* [8]. Nevertheless, our simple implementation of function fusion is enough to speed up some of Dinamica's applications dramatically.

Figure 5 illustrates some of these performance gains. In this example we are using three very simple instances of Apply and Reduce:

$$\text{Inc } m = \text{Apply } (\lambda x \ . \ x + 1) \ m$$
$$\text{Div } m = \text{Apply } (\lambda x \ . \ x/2.17) \ m$$
$$\text{Sum } m = \text{Reduce } 0 \ (\lambda(x, y) \ . \ x + y) \ m$$

In the figure we use random square matrixes of integers having sides of 5.0 K, 7.5 K and 10.0 K cells. Without fusion DinamicaVM takes 9.940 s to Div∘Inc every cell of the $10^3 \times 10^3$ matrix. Once fusion is activated, this time drops to 5.222 s. In the case of Reduce, gains are of similar nature. It takes us 7.294 s to Sum ∘ inc the matrix with 10 K rows without fusion, and 2.998 s if we use fusion. These gains are due to two factors: the elimination of intermediate data structures, and the

---

[4] Prefetching is part of the implementation of Window; it does not require any program transformation.

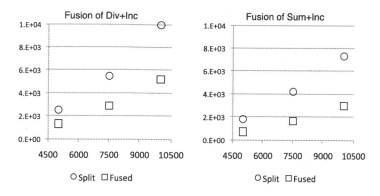

Fig. 5. Example of fusion. The Apply operator is always the increment function, and the Reduce operator is the sum of integers.

improved locality. Concerning the first factor, fusion automatically eliminates the need to copy the map that the leftmost Apply produces. As for locality, the input map will be traversed only once instead of twice. Indeed, only one iteration is necessary for any sequence of applications of the Apply functor, e.g.: apply f_1 (... (apply f_n m) ...) = apply $(f_1 \circ ... \circ f_n)$ m.

Fusion's improvements are proportional to the complexity of the operator used in Apply or Reduce. The more complex is the computation used inside these functors, less performance gains we observe. For instance, consider the following composition: Apply Normalize (apply calcSlope m). In this example, Normalize is a simple linear function of the input value, but the calcSlope operation is a substantially more complex functor present in the Dinamica EGO library. It applies a Reduce over the output of a Window for each index in the input map. For a 7500×7500 input map, fusion gives us 6 % of speedup in this example.

4.2   Window Optimizations

Window is a heavily used functor; thus, it is natural that it be optimized. DinamicaVM applies two optimizations on Window: prefetching and unrolling. The latter is only applicable on 3×3 instances of Window. Prefetching avoids unnecessary trips to main memory in order to collect the pieces of a squared window view. Unrolling removes unnecessary control flow from the most common type of view that we have observed in Dinamica's applications.

Prefetching: most of the applications that use Window slide it over an image in row-major order, that is, starting from the upper-left corner of an image, and going to its lower-right corner. This pattern is so common because it is the default order in which Apply and Reduce evaluate the elements of a map. Our optimizer ensures that each cell of a Window is read only once from main memory, if Window is used in that way. To ensure this property, we *pre-fetch* the lines that will be traversed by Window.

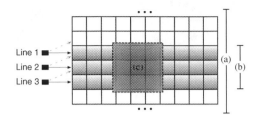

Fig. 6. The three-lines cache. The dashed arrows show line pointers in the previous iteration of Window. The solid arrows show the pointers in the current iteration. (a) Input map. (b) Cached lines. (c) Center of 3×3 window.

Figure 6 illustrates this approach for a 3×3 instance of Window. In this example, each time Window is called, it reads nine elements of the input map. Instead of fetching this data when Window is created, we pre-fetch three entire lines of the map, and let Window slide on these lines. Once Window reaches the rightmost border of the image, we discard the topmost line, and read one line more from main memory. If Window works with submatrices of n rows, then we should, in principle, keep n lines in cache. However, most of the applications available in the Dinamica's ecosystem work with 3×3 windows. Thus, we chose to work with only three lines at a time. Consequently, larger instances of Window may lead to multiple trips to the main memory. The prefetching is only necessary for maps that cannot fit entirely in the L0 cache. In the absence of this optimization, a $n \times n$ Window causes each – non-border – map cell to be read n^2 times. Usually data in the same row of Window are fetched only once to the L0 cache; however, data may be fetched more times if it happens to be read as part of different rows of Window.

Performance Improvement Due to Pre-fetching: Figure 7(a) shows the performance of three different instances of an image smoothing algorithm. The algorithm uses a 3×3 convolution matrix that does simple average to implement smoothing. The smoothing filter returns, for a given cell i, the average of all the immediate neighbours of i plus i itself. The three instances of the algorithm are:

– **Library** – the algorithm was implemented using a monolithic filter available in Dinamica's library.
– **DVM - No Opt** – our algorithm, built as the following combination of functors:
   Smooth $m =$ Apply ((Reduce Average) ∘ Window) m
– **DVM - Prefetching** – the previous implementation, with prefetching enabled in DinamicaVM.

Fig. 7(a) varies the number of times that the image is smoothed. Each time requires one application of the smoothing algorithm. Our optimization speeded up Window by a factor that reached 3.9x for 40 applications of the smoothing algorithm. It even surpassed the library component, which has a much more monolithic design. Our optimized version of image smoothing is 1.7x faster.

Unrolling: the most used type of Window is a 3×3 squared view of a map, with anchor in the center. Because this pattern is so common, we use a special implementation of it, which has no control flow. This implementation reads a chunk of memory that is large enough to fit each one of the nine indices to be processed. It then divides this memory into nine pieces, and fills up the positions in the map view with them. The size of memory that must be read is determined by the ahead-of-time compiler, before Window is invoked, but after the type of its input is already known.

Figure 7(b) shows the performance gains obtained due to unrolling and prefetching when applied on the implementation of Conway's Game of Life. This application was discussed in Sect. 2. To provide some perspective to the reader, we show the runtime of the implementation of Conway's automaton in Dinamica 2.4, before the virtual machine was released. In this case, the game is implemented with a set of functors from the library. The series "VM Base" shows our application running on the virtual machine without either prefetching or unrolling. In this case, DinamicaVM is 59 % slower than Dinamica v2.4's implementation of Conway's game. However, once we turn on optimizations, we see substantial gains: Unrolling already puts DinamicaVM's times on pair with v2.4's results. And the combination of unrolling and prefetching makes us 57 % faster than the old version of Dinamica. In other words, the two optimizations makes our virtual machine 3.6x faster.

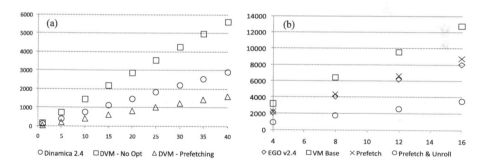

Fig. 7. (a) Performance gain due to prefetching in an image smoother. (b) Performance gains in Conway's Game of Life (Sect. 2) due to unrolling and prefetching. X-axis is data-size (image size or number of generations), and Y-axis is time, in msecs.

5   Related Work

Other Geomodeling Tools: There exist many different tools that support the development of land use models. Some of them enjoy commercial success; others are popular in the academia. We are aware of four frameworks having a moderate to large user base that might compete with Dinamica in the geomodeling niche:

ArcGis[5], Idrisi[6], and PCRaster[7]. A direct comparison between all these tools is not possible, because they use different algorithms to perform simulations. Furthermore, there is not a common benchmark suite that they all can handle. Nevertheless, there exist a few limited studies comparing some of these tools. As an example, Pérez-Vega *et al.* [15] have compared Dinamica and Idrisi, not from a performance perspective, but from the point of view of the accuracy of each modeling algorithm. Dinamica is substantially faster, and more accurate in some situations. Idrisi's algorithm, based on neural networks, is more accurate in others. We have re-implemented one of the models from the Idrisi 32 v.2 tutorial (land use map (`worcwest`), source map (`newplant`) and destination map (`powerline`)), in both Dinamica EGO v1.8 and ArcGis 9.3. Figure 8 shows the result. The goal of this model is to find an optimum pathway in a map, given the cost of traversing the terrain. We have experimented with different resolutions: 5 meters (2,880 × 2,880 cells) and 15 meters (960 × 960 cells). Dinamica uses an iterative algorithm, which we might stop after a few passes over the map, or we might iterate until reaching an optimal solution. We did not perceive visual difference between the path found within 3 iterations or Dinamica's optimal solution. For the 15 meters models, Dinamica's 3-passes solution was 120 times faster than Idrisi's and 264 times faster than ArcGis's. For the 5 m version, Dinamica's 3-passes model took 46 s, while neither Idrisi nor ArcGis were able to run the model. This difference is larger in multicore computers. For example, on a laptop DELL Alienware with 8 cores, Dinamica's 2-passes solution takes less than 2 s to process the 15-m model, almost doubling performance. In this same setup, the computing time of the other GIS platforms increased due to disk accesses. Mas et al. [12] compared Dinamica EGO in relation to CLUE-S and GEOMOD.

Dataflow Programming Languages. Dinamica EGO implements a dataflow programming environment. Quoting Daniel Hils [10], "The central concept of the data flow model is that a program can be represented by a directed graph where nodes represent functions and where arcs represent the flow of data between functions." The idea of representing computation as graphs has been studied at

Modeling method	15 m (960^2)	5 m $(2,880^2)$
Dinamica, 2 iterations	3 sec	31 sec
Dinamica, 3 iterations	5 sec	46 sec
Dinamica, optimum	38 sec	6 min 6 sec
Idrisi MacroModeler 32 v.2	10 min	–
ArcGIS ModelBuilder 9.3	22 min	–

Fig. 8. A comparison between three different tools.

---

[5] http://www.esri.com/software/arcgis.

[6] http://clarklabs.org/.

[7] http://pcraster.geo.uu.nl/.

least as early as 1966 [1]. However, we are not aware of any data flow language that supports geomodeling in particular.

6   Conclusion

This paper has presented DinamicaVM, the virtual machine that supports the execution of applications built on top of the Dinamica EGO geo-scientific framework. DinamicaVM differs from other virtual machines, such as Oracle's JVM or Microsoft's .NET, in a number of ways. In particular, DinamicaVM is not a general purpose virtual machine: it is tailored to run applications that process very large images representing cartographic maps. Furthermore, as we saw in the paper, DinamicaVM has a high-level instruction set, which includes components borrowed from functional programming, such as *map* (e.g., Apply) and Reduce. Dinamica EGO is open source, and is available on-line.

This work lets us draw conclusions which are also valid to other data-flow and functional programming environments. First, it is possible to design and implement a very expressive instruction set, and still ensure that these instructions can be interpreted efficiently. Key to this efficiency are the optimizations that we apply after type-checking the application, but before loading it up. Second, it is possible to make the most of the specific nature of applications that will run on the virtual machine with very positive results. In our case, the virtual machine is customized to handle large images and tables, which are typical in geosciences. This observation lets us believe that the techniques currently available in DinamicaVM can be of use in other systems that process large images.

References

1. Bohm, C., Jacopini, G.: Flow diagrams, turing machines and languages with only two formation rules. Commun. ACM **9**(5), 366–371 (1966)
2. Cytron, R., Ferrante, J., Rosen, B.K., Wegman, M.N., Zadeck, F.K.: Efficiently computing static single assignment form and the control dependence graph. TOPLAS **13**(4), 451–490 (1991)
3. Dean, J., Ghemawat, S.: Mapreduce: simplified data processing on large clusters. Commun. ACM **51**(1), 107–113 (2008)
4. Eastman, J.R.: Pushbroom algorithms for calculating distances in raster grids. In: Auto-Carto, pp. 288–297. ASPRS and ACSM (1989)
5. Ferreira, B.M., ao Pereira, F.M.Q., Rodrigues, H., Soares-Filho, B.S.: Optimizing a geomodeling domain specific language. In: Simposio Brasileiro de Linguagens de Programacao. Sociedade Brasileira de Computacao (2012)
6. Gamma, E., Helm, R., Johnson, R., Vlissides, J.: Design Patterns: Elements of Reusable Object-oriented Software. Addison-Wesley Longman Publishing Co. Inc., Boston (1995)
7. Gardner, M.: Mathematical games - the fantastic combination of John conway's new solitaire game life. Sci. Am. **1**(223), 120–123 (1970)
8. Gill, A., Launchbury, J., Peyton Jones, S.L.: A short cut to deforestation. In: Proceedings of the Conference on Functional Programming Languages and Computer Architecture, FPCA 1993, pp. 223–232. ACM, New York (1993). http://doi.acm.org/10.1145/165180.165214

9. Hajek, F., Ventresca, M.J., Scriven, J., Castro, A.: Regime-building for REDD+: evidence from a cluster of local initiatives in south-eastern Peru. Environ. Sci. Policy **14**(2), 201–215 (2011)
10. Hils, D.D.: Visual languages and computing survey: data flow visual programming languages. J. Visual Lang. Comput. **3**, 69–101 (1992)
11. Huong, H.T.L., Pathirana, A.: Urbanization and climate change impacts on future urban flood risk in can tho city, Vietnam. Hydrol. Earth Syst. Sci. Discuss. **8**(6), 10781–10824 (2011)
12. Mas, J.F., Kolb, M., Paegelow, M., Camacho Olmedo, M.T., Houet, T.: Inductive pattern-based land use/cover change models: a comparison of four software packages. Environ. Model. Softw. **51**, 94–111 (2014). http://dx.doi.org/10.1016/j.envsoft.2013.09.010
13. Nepstad, D., Soares-Filho, B., Merry, F., Lima, A., Moutinho, P., Carter, J., Bowman, M., Cattaneo, A., Rodrigues, H., Schwartzman, S., McGrath, D., Stickler, C., Lubowski, R., Piris-Cabeza, P., Rivero, S., Alencar, A., Almeida, O., Stella, O.: The end of deforestation in the Brazilian amazon. Science **326**, 1350–1351 (2009)
14. Nielson, H.R., Nielson, F.: Semantics with Applications - A Formal Introduction. Wiley, New York (1992)
15. Pérez-Vega, A., Mas, J.F., Ligmann-Zielinska, A.: Comparing two approaches to land use/cover change modeling and their implications for the assessment of biodiversity loss in a deciduous tropical forest. Environ. Model. Softw. **29**(1), 11–23 (2012)
16. Soares-Filho, B., Nepstad, D., Curran, L., Cerqueira, G., Garcia, R., Ramos, C., Voll, E., McDonald, A., Lefebvre, P., Schlesinger, P.: Modelling conservation in the Amazon basin. Nature **440**, 520–523 (2006)
17. Soares-Filho, B., Pennachin, C., Cerqueira, G.: Dinamica - a stochastic cellular automata model designed to simulate the landscape dynamics in an Amazonian colonization frontier. Ecol. Model. **154**, 217–235 (2002)
18. Soares-Filho, B., Rajo, R., Macedo, M., Carneiro, A., Costa, W., Coe, M., Rodrigues, H., Alencar, A.: Cracking Brazil's forest code. Science **344**(6182), 363–364 (2014). http://www.sciencemag.org/content/344/6182/363.short
19. Thapa, R.B., Murayama, Y.: Urban growth modeling of Kathmandu metropolitan region, Nepal. Comput. Environ. Urban Syst. **35**(1), 25–34 (2011)
20. Tomlin, C.D.: Geographic Information Systems and Cartographic Modelling. Prentice-Hall, Englewood Cliffs (1990)
21. Wadler, P.: Deforestation: transforming programs to eliminate trees. Theor. Comput. Sci. **73**(2), 231–248 (1988)

Go Model and Object Oriented Programming

Haiyang Liu$^{(\boxtimes)}$ and Zongyan Qiu

LMAM and Department of Informatics, School of Mathematics,
Peking University, Beijing, China
{liuhaiyang,zyqiu}@pku.edu.cn

Abstract. Go is a contemporary language aiming to support OO programming where the core OO feature, inheritance, is intentionally excluded. Go uses the concepts of embedding and interface to provide its object model. To understand the design of Go and its consequences, we develop a simple Go-like model language, mini-Go, which abstracts Go's interface-based OO features. The formal defined type system and semantics are given. In addition, we propose an even simpler language μGo where the feature of pointers is further removed. We demonstrate that μGo is as expressive in OO as the original language with pointers, which provides a uniform model for Go-like OO programming. We investigate the OO model of the Go-like languages using μGo in detail, point out that the absence of open recursion brings difficulties in OO design, and then propose a novel design pattern to mimic the open recursion feature to overcome the difficulties.

Keywords: Programming language · Object Oriented · Go

1 Introduction

The Object Oriented (OO) programming facilities play an important role in the development of programming languages and software engineering practice. Class/Inheritance are core in mainstream OO languages to support OO programming necessities, e.g., encapsulation, subtyping, polymorphism, etc. Additionally, OO facilities, like class, composition, inheritance, and other OO facilities are also heavily used in design patterns, which can, in many useful cases, give clean and neat solutions [1].

Although class and inheritance are basic language features for OO programming, sometimes they are misused or overused in practice, and that leads to inflexible or too complicated designs. By recognizing this problem, Gamma *et al.* [1] proposed two principles for reusable OO design:

- Program to an interface, not an implementation.
- Favor object composition over class inheritance.

Both aim to restrict the use of class and inheritance in practice. These principles are reflected in the late OO languages and program designs. Java introduces the interfaces – a special kind of abstract classes – and use it in its standard library

© Springer International Publishing Switzerland 2015
A. Pardo and S.D. Swierstra (Eds.): SBLP 2015, LNCS 9325, pp. 59–74, 2015.
DOI: 10.1007/978-3-319-24012-1_5

to support mix-in paradigm to enhance the flexibility. A statistic research on practical Java projects [2] shows that more interfaces than classes are used in projects, while most inheritance is shallow (and then restricted).

Those lead people to think about the OO language design which emphasizes more on the interfaces rather than classes, composition rather than inheritance, and simple inheritance/implementation rather than complicated type hierarchy. The Go programming language developed by Google reflects this trend.

Go [3] is a relatively new language designed by Rob Pike, Ken Thompson, and others. It was conceived in late 2007 and published in November 2009. Go is a compiled, concurrent, garbage-collected, statically typed language designed to solve problems introduced by multi-core processors, networked systems, massive computation clusters, and the web programming model [4].

Go supports OO programming in a novel way. A typical OO language, e.g. Java or C#, supports OO via the concepts of class and inheritance. In contrast, Go has no class, nor inheritance. It uses *embed* types and *interfaces* to support OO programming. The embed types enable code reuse, and interfaces enable polymorphism. Go designers believe that eliminating inheritance makes the language more lightweight and easier to use, and still flexible and expressive [5].

We are interested in how the embedding and special interface facilities of Go affect its expressiveness and conciseness for OO programming; and what the semantics of Go's object oriented model is with respect to the subtle difference between interfaces of Go and other languages. Then we conduct this work. First we build a concise model language out of Go in Sect. 3, and defines its type system and semantics; then in Sect. 4, we found that the pointers can be removed to have μGo, which is a simpler Go-like language. Moreover, we find out some inherent weak points of Go model in supporting OO programming in this study, and it will be discussed in Sect. 5.

2   Go: A First Glance

Initially, this section gives a brief introduction of Go with focus on its OOP related features.

The following interface definitions are taken from Go's standard package `io`:

```
package io
type Writer interface {                     type WriteCloser interface {
    Write(p []byte) (n int, err error)          Writer
}                                               Closer
type Closer interface {                     }
    Close() error
}
```

The code seems similar to the interface definitions in Java. Here `Writer` and `Closer` are declared as two simple interfaces where each has only one method, and `WriteCloser` extends (in term of Go, embeds) both of them.

However, compared with Java or C#, interfaces in Go play different roles, have different semantics and make the implementation relation implicit. Interface types have their own values in Go. An interface variables holds an interface value, which includes the actual value with its runtime type, thus it is more like an object in Java or C#. A type T implements an interface I, if T provides all methods declared in I, which is so-called "duck typing" in Go. For example, structure `os.File` and interface `net.Conn` below both implement `io.WriteCloser`, simply because they provide all methods declared in `Write` and `Close`. No explicit declaration is necessary.

```
package net
type Conn interface {
    Read(b []byte) (n int, err error)
    Write(b []byte) (n int, err error)
    Close() error
    LocalAddr() Addr
    // ......
}
```

```
package os
type File struct {
    *file
}
func (f *File) Close() error { ... }
func (f *File) Read(b []byte)
                   (n int, err error){...}
// ......
```

A function with a `io.WriteCloser` parameter will accept an argument of type `net.Conn` or `os.File`. This enables dynamic polymorphism. If we define:

```
func copyAndClose(w io.WriteCloser, r io.Reader) {
    io.Copy(w, r)
    if err := w.Close(); err != nil {
        log.Println("Error closing", err)
    }
}
```

Both `copyAndClose(fileA,fileB)` and `copyAndClose(connA,fileB)` are valid.

People announce that Go supports OOP in a special way [5]. However, we want to clarify what does it mean that Go supports OOP, and whether or not this OO model possesses some inherent limitations, and if it does, whether we can overcome the limitations.

Pierce summarized some main features to identify OOP [6, Sect. 18.1], and we list them here with some discussions related to Go language:

1. Multiple representations of operations. When an operation is invoked via a variable on an object, the object itself determines what code gets executed. This is also called *dynamic dispatch*, and is the most important characteristic of OO. In Go, a variable with an interface type I can preserve an interface value that refer to an object of any type that implements I, and the interface value determines what code to be executed.
2. Encapsulation. The internal representation of objects is hidden from the client code. Go provides only package level encapsulation mechanism.
3. Subtyping. The type of an object is just the set of names and types of its operations. It implies a natural subtype relation, that an object satisfies an interface I if it satisfies an interface J whose operations is a superset of I's. Go's interface feature provides a perfect pattern of subtyping mechanism.
4. Inheritance. Inheritance between classes in OO languages is a mechanism for code reuse. Although Go has no class, its embedding mechanism for structures and interfaces enables code reuse without introducing complex type hierarchy. This embedding mechanism is just similar to inheritance in the sense of [6].
5. Open recursion. Most OO languages have a special variable called `self` or `this`, which allows a method in a class to invoke methods that are defined

later in a subclass. Go does not have this feature. Methods in Go need to declare a receiver variable explicitly, and the variable is not late-bound.

As pointed out above, *embedding* and *interface* are the keys in Go's OO model, which are main features to support code reuse, while the interfaces support polymorphism. However, obviously some regular features in common OO languages are absent in Go, e.g. the type hierarchy and late-bound method receiver. Do these absences affect Go's expressiveness and conciseness in OOP? We will discuss these topics in detail below.

3   Mini-Go: A Model Language for Go OO Model

To conduct a rigorous study on Go's object model in detail, we need a formal defined language. We select a subset of Go related to OO programming and name it mini-Go, as a basis for our investigation.

$$
\begin{array}{lll}
Pr ::= \texttt{bool} \mid \ldots & & \text{[primitive type]} \\
T ::= Pr \mid I \mid S \mid *T & & \text{[type]} \\
b ::= \texttt{true} \mid \texttt{false} \mid e == e \mid \neg b \mid b \wedge b \mid b \vee b & & \text{[boolean expression]} \\
le ::= v \mid v.a \mid *v & & \text{[lvalue expression]} \\
e ::= \texttt{nil} \mid b \mid le \mid \&le & & \text{[expression]} \\
c ::= \texttt{skip} \mid le = e \mid le = \texttt{new}(S) \mid\mid x = v.(T) \mid x = v.m(\bar{e}) \mid & & \text{[statement]} \\
\quad \texttt{return}\ e \mid c;c \mid \texttt{if}\ b\ \{c\}\ \texttt{else}\ \{c\} \mid \texttt{while}\ b\ \{c\} & & \\
msig ::= m(\overline{v\ T})\ T & & \text{[method signature]} \\
md ::= \texttt{func}\ (r\ S)\ msig\ \{\overline{\texttt{var}\ v\ T}; c\} & & \text{[method definition]} \\
\quad \texttt{func}\ (r\ *S)\ msig\ \{\overline{\texttt{var}\ v\ T}; c\} & & \\
sd ::= \texttt{type}\ S\ \texttt{struct}\ \{\overline{S}; \overline{I}; \overline{a\ T}\} & & \text{[struct definition]} \\
id ::= \texttt{type}\ I\ \texttt{interface}\ \{\overline{I}; \overline{msig}\} & & \text{[interface definition]} \\
prog ::= \overline{id}\ \overline{sd}\ \overline{md} & & \text{[program]}
\end{array}
$$

Fig. 1. Syntax of mini-Go

The syntax of mini-Go is given in Fig. 1, where I and S are interface and structure type names, respectively; v, x are variable names; a is a data field of a structure; r is the receiver of a method (like this in Java and C++, but no special name required in Go). We use overlined terms to denote finite comma-separated sequences of zero or more elements.

We take only bool here as a primitive data type in the syntax, while other primitive types can be added without difficulty. Many types of Go—arrays, slices, maps, functions, and channels—are omitted in this work, simply because they are less-related to our main subject. Here are only 3 composite types: structures, interfaces, and pointers. However, unlike in Go [3], here we assume that nil has a special type Null for the completeness of typing.

We adopt restricted side-effect free expressions in mini-Go. This is not substantial. Complicated expressions, possibly with side effects, can be encoded with the help of assignments and auxiliary variables. For example, $f(x) + g(y)$ in Go can be encoded with $a + b$ after $a = f(x); b = g(y)$. We import only some basic statements for sequential programming, where skip denotes the empty statement for clarity.

A method signature does not contain the type of its receiver, that simplifies the description of the method set of interfaces. However, unlike [3], here the signature contains the method name. Non-method functions in Go are omitted in mini-Go. This does not affect the expressiveness since every function can be treated as a method of a dummy structure type. All variables in mini-Go are declared at the beginning of methods and there is exactly one return statement at the end. These simplify the semantics of mini-Go.

In addition, structures and interfaces are declared at the beginning of a program, and their scope is assumed to be the whole program. Methods are defined at the global scope. At last, a mini-Go program is just a sequence of interfaces, structures, and method declarations.

Mini-Go takes the similar typing rules and semantics as Go. Furthermore, a valid mini-Go program is also a valid Go program (except for skip) which has the same behavior. For example, the sketch codes given in Sect. 2 are all valid in mini-Go. From these, we see how mini-Go supports OO programming.

The detail of mini-Go is given in the technical report [7]. We list some important typing and semantics rules below with the focus on the OO behaviors.

$$\frac{T \in \Gamma_{\mathsf{s}} \cup *\Gamma_{\mathsf{s}} \cup \Gamma_{\mathsf{i}} \qquad I \in \Gamma_{\mathsf{i}} \qquad \Gamma_{\mathsf{m}}(I) \subseteq \Gamma_{\mathsf{m}}(T)}{\Gamma \vdash I \prec T}$$

$$\frac{\Gamma \vdash T_1 \prec T_2}{\Gamma \vdash T_1 \preceq T_2} \qquad \frac{T \in \Gamma_{\mathsf{t}}}{\Gamma \vdash T \preceq T} \qquad \frac{T \in \Gamma_{\mathsf{t}} \setminus (\{\mathtt{Null}, \mathtt{bool}\} \cup \Gamma_{\mathsf{s}})}{\Gamma \vdash T \preceq \mathtt{Null}}$$

$$\frac{\Gamma, C, m \vdash le : T_1 \qquad \Gamma, C, m \vdash e : T_2 \qquad \Gamma \vdash T_1 \preceq T_2}{\Gamma, C, m \vdash le = e : \mathbf{com}}$$

$$\frac{\Gamma, C, m \vdash v : T_0 \qquad \Gamma_{\mathsf{m}}(T_0)(m_0) = (\overline{v_i \mapsto T_i}) \mapsto T}{\forall i \cdot (\Gamma, C, m \vdash e_i : T_i' \quad T_i \preceq T_i') \qquad \Gamma, C, m \vdash x : T' \qquad \Gamma \vdash T' \preceq T}{\Gamma, C, m \vdash x = v.m_0(\overline{e_i}) : \mathbf{com}}$$

Fig. 2. Selected typing rules for mini-Go

3.1   Typing

With a static environment Γ of the mini-Go program, we use $\Gamma, C, m \vdash e : T$ to assert that expression e has type T in method m of composite type C, where C may be a structure type or a pointer type to a structure; and use $\Gamma, C, m \vdash c : \mathbf{com}$ to assert that statement c is well-formed in method m of type C. For convenience, we use Γ_{s}, Γ_{i}, and Γ_{t} to represent the names of the structures, the interfaces, the types, respectively. And we use $\Gamma_{\mathsf{e}}(T)$ to denote types *embedded* in T. In addition, Γ_{m} maps a structure, a pointer to structure, or interface type T to its *method set*, $\Gamma_{\mathsf{m}}(T)$, which includes all T's method names and signatures.

The method set of pointer $*S$ includes the methods defined for both S and $*S$, where S is a structure type. And $\Gamma_v(T)(m)$ and $\Gamma_b(T)(m)$ are the local variables and method body of method m of type T respectively.

Figure 2 lists some important typing rules, while the complete set of rules can be found in the technical report [7].

$\Gamma, S, m \vdash$ stype$(e) = T$ is denoted as $\Gamma, S, m \vdash e : T$ for convenience, and we just write stype$(e) = T$ when the static environment is clear from the context.

Supposing that I is an interface and T is a composite type (structure, pointer, or interface), we say that T *implements* I, denoted as $\Gamma \vdash I \prec T$, if I's method set is a subset of T's. This is defined by the first rule in Fig. 2. The implementation relation shows that mini-Go has a structural type system for interface types, which is the so-called "duck typing" feature in Go.

In mini-Go, a right value expression e can be assigned to a left value expression le of type T, just in cases that:

- e has type T, say $\Gamma, S, m \vdash e : T$.
- T is an interface type, and T is implemented by the type of e.
- e is nil, and T is an interface type or pointer type.

We now define the type *compatibility* relation $\preceq$, which is the reflexive transitive closure of implementation relation $\prec$. Meanwhile, we define that Null type is compatible with all interface types and pointer types as in Fig. 2.

We also give rules for the well-typedness of assignment statements and method invocation. For the method invocation, firstly, the method signature is found through the type of receiver, then the types of actual arguments' types are checked to be compatible with formal arguments' types, at last the assignment of return value is checked. The receiver type T_0 here can be a structure, a pointer to a structure, or an interface.

3.2 Semantics

Now we define a structural operational semantics [8] for mini-Go as a configuration transformation. The configurations of mini-Go programs are defined as:

$$Configure = (Statements \times Stack \times Heap) \cup (Stack \times Heap)$$

In a configuration, $\eta \in Statements$ is the current code to be executed. A local variable stack $\sigma \in Stack$ is a list of frame $s \colon ID \rightharpoonup_{fin} Addr$, which is a finite map from identifiers to heap addresses, where ID is a set of names, and $Addr$ is the heap address space. To be concise, supposing that $\sigma = s :: \sigma'$, we define

$$\sigma(x) \triangleq s(x) \qquad \sigma[x \mapsto v] \triangleq s[x \mapsto v] = s \setminus \{x \mapsto \_\} \cup \{x \mapsto v\}$$

where x is a variable name, v is a value, and $s[x \mapsto v]$ denotes the new frame after updating the frame s with the value v for the variable x.

At last, an object heap $h \in Heap$ is a finite partial map:

$$h \colon Addr \rightharpoonup_{fin} Value$$

where $Value = PrimValue \cup Addr \cup Value^{ID} \cup (Type \times Value)$

Here $Type$ is the set of types. Set $Value$ is divided into four disjoint subsets: (1) the primitive value set, $PrimValue$ (true and false for bool, for example);

$$[\text{Asn}] \ \frac{\sigma, h \vDash \mathsf{ref}(le) = addr, \mathsf{assign}(le, e) = val}{(le = e, \sigma, h) \rightsquigarrow (\sigma, h[addr \mapsto val])}$$

$$[\text{Inv}] \ \frac{\begin{array}{c} \mathsf{lookup}(\mathsf{dtype}(v), \mathsf{dref}(v), m) = (vars, c_m, val) \\ vars = \{r \mapsto T, ret \mapsto V, \overline{a_i \mapsto U_i}, \overline{v_k \mapsto T_k}\} \\ \sigma_m = \{r \mapsto addr_0, ret \mapsto addr_r, \overline{a_i \mapsto addr_i}, \overline{v_k \mapsto addr_k}\} :: \sigma, \quad addr_{0,r,i,k} \notin \mathrm{dom}(h) \\ h_m = h \cup \{addr_0 \mapsto val, \overline{addr_i \mapsto \mathsf{assign}(a_i, e_i)}\} \\ (c_m, \sigma_m, h_m) \rightsquigarrow (\sigma', h') \qquad \sigma', h' \vDash \mathsf{assign}(x, ret) = rval \end{array}}{(x = v.m(\overline{e_i}), \sigma, h) \rightsquigarrow (\sigma, h'[\sigma(x) \mapsto rval])}$$

Fig. 3. Selected semantic rules for mini-Go

(2) the address value set, for pointers; (3) the structure value set, where each object $o: ID \rightharpoonup_{\text{fin}} Value$ is a finite partial map from names of data fields to their values; and (4) the interface value set, $Type \times Value$, in which every interface value stores an object with its dynamic type.

In mini-Go, an interface variable holds an interface value, which includes the actual object with its runtime type. Unlike the class based OO languages, an object does not know its runtime type in mini-Go, therefore the type information in the interface value is necessary to support dynamic dispatching.

Mini-Go has only local variables. A variable holds the reference (heap address) of an object, and the actual object is stored in the heap. In addition, we suppose that there is an offset function offset: $Addr \times ID \rightarrow Addr$. For address a of a structure of type T and a field name f, $\mathsf{offset}(a, f)$ gives address a_f of the field. We ignore the details of offset, which can be easily built in practice.

The evaluation of a value expression is a routine work, thus we only pay attention to evaluating a left-value expression and its address. For any left-value expression e, we can get its address by function ref:

$$\sigma, h \vDash \mathsf{ref}(e) = \begin{cases} \sigma(v) & e \text{ is } v, \\ \mathsf{offset}(\sigma(v), a) & e \text{ is } v.a, \\ h(\sigma(v)) & e \text{ is } *v. \end{cases}$$

Then it is easy to define the evaluation function for left-value expressions:

$$\sigma, h \vDash \mathsf{eval}(\&e) = \mathsf{ref}(e), \mathsf{eval}(e) = h(\mathsf{ref}(e)).$$

And we can now define the functions of dynamic type and of reference to dynamic value for convenience:

$$\sigma, h \vDash \mathsf{dtype}(e), \mathsf{dref}(e) = \begin{cases} \mathsf{stype}(e), \mathsf{ref}(e), & \mathsf{stype}(e) \notin \Gamma_i, \\ T, \mathsf{offset}(\mathsf{ref}(e), val) & \mathsf{stype}(e) \in \Gamma_i, \text{ where } \mathsf{eval}(e) = (T, val). \end{cases}$$

where the dynamic type and value of an expression of non-interface type are its static type and the evaluated value respectively, and the dynamic type and value of an expression of interface type are stored in the interface value.

We list in Fig. 3 only semantic rules for the assignment and method invocation, while the other rules are given in the technical report [7].

There are two situations for assignment and parameter passing: when we assign a non-interface value to an interface variable, we need to make a new interface value from the original value and its type first, then do the assignment

$$\text{lookup: } \textit{Type} \times \textit{Addr} \times \textit{ID} \rightharpoonup_{\text{fin}} \textit{Vars} \times \textit{Body} \times \textit{Value}.$$

$$\text{lookup}(T, addr, m) = \begin{cases} (\Gamma_v(T)(m), \Gamma_b(T)(m), val), & \Gamma_b(T)(m) \neq \bot, \\ \text{lookup}(T', \text{ref}(val'), m), & \Gamma_b(T)(m) = \bot, I \in \Gamma_i \cap \Gamma_e(T), \end{cases}$$

where $\qquad\qquad\qquad\qquad\qquad\qquad\qquad\qquad \text{offset}(addr, I) = (T', val').$

$$val = \begin{cases} h(addr), & \Gamma_r(T)(m) = T, \\ h(h(addr)), & \Gamma_r(T)(m) = *T, \\ addr, & *\Gamma_r(T)(m) = T, \\ h(\text{offset}(addr, T_e)), & T \neq \Gamma_r(T)(m) = T_e \in \Gamma_e(T). \end{cases}$$

Fig. 4. Method lookup function of mini-Go

or parameters passing; otherwise, we just assign the value to the destination variable as usual. To simplify the semantic rules, we introduce an assignment function to denote the value to be assigned in statement $le = e$:

$$\sigma, h \vDash \text{assign}(le, e) = \begin{cases} \text{eval}(e), & \text{stype}(le) \notin \Gamma_i \text{ or stype}(e) \in \Gamma_i \\ (\text{stype}(e), \text{eval}(e)), & \text{stype}(le) \in \Gamma_i, \text{stype}(e) \notin \Gamma_i. \end{cases}$$

Then we can unify the different cases in one rule [Asn].

The rule for method invocation is a bit complicated, because we mimic Go to use different strategies to lookup the method body for pointer, structure and interface variables. We have a formal definition for a lookup function which reflects the corresponding rule of Go (Fig. 4). lookup takes the dynamic type $\text{dtype}(v)$ of variable v, the reference $\text{dref}(v)$ to the dynamic value of v, and the method name m as parameters, and determines the local variables $vars$ of m, its body code c_m, and the receiver value val. Because of embedding structures and interfaces in mini-Go, the lookup function is defined recursively:

1. If method m is defined in type T, we can extract the method body directly. Mini-Go does not distinguish pointers and non-pointers receivers when calling methods. Pointers are automatically dereferenced for non-pointer receivers, and non-pointer variables' addresses are passed to pointer receivers.
2. If method m is defined in an embedding non-interface type T_e, we can also extract the method body directly, and get the receiver value $h(\text{offset}(addr, T_e)) = \text{eval}(v.T_e)$ as the embedded T_e field of v.
3. If method m is defined in an embedding interface type I, we recursively lookup the method body from dynamic type and value of the embedded interface value $val(I)$.

Having the method body, a method invocation is split into several stages: evaluating actual arguments, establishing new method's environment, executing the method body, and assigning the return value to the result variable. In rule [Inv], local variables are $vars$, and the environment of the method is σ_m and h_m, where $addr_0, addr_r, addr_i, addr_k \notin \text{dom}(h)$ are new allocated heap addresses. We can see that all the arguments, including the receiver, are passed by value.

3.3   Redundancies of Mini-Go and Go

By building a formal model for mini-Go, we find that there are some clear redundancies in the design of Go. Most importantly, Go provides two concepts

$$Pr ::= \textbf{bool} \mid \ldots \qquad\qquad\qquad\qquad\qquad \text{[primitive type]}$$
$$T ::= Pr \mid I \mid S \qquad\qquad\qquad\qquad\qquad\qquad \text{[type]}$$
$$b ::= \textbf{true} \mid \textbf{false} \mid e == e \mid \neg b \mid b \wedge b \mid b \vee b \qquad \text{[boolean expression]}$$
$$e ::= b \mid \textbf{nil} \mid v \qquad\qquad\qquad\qquad\qquad\qquad \text{[expression]}$$
$$c ::= \textbf{skip} \mid x = e \mid v.a = x \mid x = v.a \mid v = \textbf{new}(S) \mid x = v.(T) \mid \qquad \text{[statement]}$$
$$\quad x = v.m(\overline{e}) \mid \textbf{return } e \mid c; c \mid \textbf{if } b \ \{c\} \ \textbf{else } \{c\} \mid \textbf{while } b \ \{c\}$$
$$msig ::= m(\overline{v\ T})\ T \qquad\qquad\qquad\qquad\qquad \text{[method signature]}$$
$$md ::= \textbf{func } (r\ S)\ msig\ \{\textbf{var } v\ T; c\} \qquad\qquad \text{[method definition]}$$
$$sd ::= \textbf{type } S\ \textbf{struct } \{\overline{S}; \overline{I}; \overline{a\ T}\} \qquad\qquad \text{[struct definition]}$$
$$id ::= \textbf{type } I\ \textbf{interface } \{\overline{I}; \overline{msig}\} \qquad\qquad \text{[interface definition]}$$
$$prog ::= \overline{id}; \overline{sd}; \overline{md} \qquad\qquad\qquad\qquad\qquad \text{[program]}$$

Fig. 5. Syntax of μGo

for the receivers to support method dispatching: *object values* and *pointers*. As is pointed in Fig. 4, when passing an object argument to a pointer parameter as a receiver, the object's address is taken and passed. Similarly, when passing a pointer argument to an value parameter as a receiver, the pointer is dereferenced to pass the object it refers:

```
type T struct{}              var v T; v = T{}
func (r T) byVal() {         var p *T; p = new(T)
}                            p.byVal()   // r gets *p
func (pr *T) byPtr() {       p.byPtr()   // pr gets p
}                            v.byVal()   // r gets v
                             v.byPtr()   // pr gets &v
```

The syntactic sugar gets more complicated when interfaces are involved. The method set of a pointer type includes the methods of its corresponding value type, but the method set of a value type does not includes those methods with a value type receiver. What's more, interface variables are assigned by value. This is confusing, and make the semantics complicated.

```
type ByVal interface {       var iv_p ByVal = p   // OK
    byVal()                  var iv_v ByVal = v   // OK, copy v
}                            var ip_p ByPtr = p   // OK
type ByPtr interface {
    byPtr()                  // ERROR: T does not implements ByPtr
}                            var ip_v ByPtr = v
```

Non-pointer receivers can always be replaced by pointer receivers, so we can change the semantics a little to pass the receiver by reference and avoid pointer types. And we can go further to change the semantics of interface variables, to allow interface variables preserving the references rather than the values of objects. This does not restrict the expressiveness of the language, but makes it possible to remove the pointer types entirely and results in a more uniform model. These observations lead to a simpler model language μGo, which will be discussed in Sect. 4.

4 μGo: A Simplified OO Model Language for Go

Now we develop an even simpler model language for Go, namely μGo, where we omit the pointers presented in Go, and change the semantics of interface variables to be references. Figure 5 gives the syntax of μGo, which is almost the same as mini-Go, except that features related to pointers are completely removed. This simplifies (and unifies) the syntax of expressions and assignments, and makes the method definitions concentrating to only one form. The receiver takes the reference semantics as we mentioned earlier, that will be defined below.

4.1   Typing μGo

We take a similar static type environment Γ as described in Sect. 3. Notations Γ_s, Γ_i, Γ_t, and Γ_m have the same meanings as in mini-Go, for the structure name set, the interface name set, the type name set, and the mapping from a type to its method set, respectively.

$$\frac{S \in \Gamma_s \quad I \in \Gamma_i \quad \Gamma_m(I) \subseteq \Gamma_m(S)}{\Gamma \vdash I \prec S} \qquad \frac{\Gamma, S, m \vdash x : T_1 \quad \Gamma, S, m \vdash e : T_2 \quad \Gamma \vdash T_1 \preceq T_2}{\Gamma, S, m \vdash x = e : \mathbf{com}}$$

$$\frac{\Gamma, S, m \vdash v : T_0 \quad \Gamma_m(S_0)(m_0) = \overline{(v_i \mapsto T_i)} \mapsto T}{\forall i \cdot \left(\Gamma, S, m \vdash e_i : T_i' \quad T_i \preceq T_i' \right) \quad \Gamma, S, m \vdash x : T' \quad \Gamma \vdash T' \preceq T}{\Gamma, S, m \vdash x = v.m_0(\overline{e_i}) : \mathbf{com}}$$

Fig. 6. Selected typing rules for μGo

In Fig. 6 we list some important typing rules for μGo. Since pointers are absent, the implementation relation $\prec$ of μGo is defined by only one rule, and the type compatibility relation $\preceq$ remains the same as in mini-Go. We also define the static type function stype for μGo as in mini-Go.

The rules for typing assignments, and the well-typedness of method invocation statement remain the same as in mini-Go. For the invocation, we get the method signature through the type of receiver, then check types of actual arguments against the types of formal parameters. At last we check the assignment of return value. The receiver type T_0 here can be a structure or an interface.

4.2   Operational Semantics

The configurations of a μGo program has the same form as in mini-Go. However, the structure of heap is different. Address values are gone in μGo as expected, and interface values now store the reference to the objects with its type, not the object itself:

$$h : Addr \rightharpoonup_{\mathrm{fin}} Value$$

$$\text{where } Value = PrimValue \cup Value^{ID} \cup (Type \times Addr)$$

$$[\mu\mathsf{Asn}]\ \frac{\sigma, h \vDash \mathsf{ref}(le) = addr, \mathsf{assign}(le, e) = val}{(le = e, \sigma, h) \rightsquigarrow (\sigma, h[addr \mapsto val])}$$

$$[\mu\mathsf{Inv}]\ \frac{\begin{array}{c} \mathsf{lookup}(\mathsf{dtype}(v), \mathsf{dref}(v), m) = (vars, c_m, addr_r) \\ vars = \left\{ r \mapsto T, ret \mapsto V, a_i \mapsto U_i, v_k \mapsto T_k \right\} \\ \sigma_m = \left\{ r \mapsto addr_0, ret \mapsto addr_r, \overline{a_i \mapsto addr_i}, \overline{v_k \mapsto addr_k} \right\} :: \sigma, \quad addr_{0,r,i,k} \notin \mathsf{dom}(h) \\ h_m = h \cup \left\{ \overline{addr_i \mapsto \mathsf{assign}(a_i, e_i)} \right\} \\ (c_m, \sigma_m, h_m) \rightsquigarrow (\sigma', h') \quad \sigma', h' \vDash \mathsf{assign}(x, ret) = rval \end{array}}{(x = v.m(\overline{e_i}), \sigma, h) \rightsquigarrow (\sigma, h'[\sigma(x) \mapsto rval])}$$

Fig. 7. Selected semantic rules of μGo

$$\mathsf{lookup}:\ Type \times Addr \times ID \rightarrow_{\mathsf{fin}} Vars \times Body \times Addr.$$

$\mathsf{lookup}(T, addr, m)$

$$= \begin{cases} (\Gamma_{\mathsf{v}}(T)(m), \Gamma_{\mathsf{b}}(T)(m), addr), & \Gamma_{\mathsf{b}}(T)(m) \neq \bot, \Gamma_{\mathsf{r}}(T)(m) = T, \\ (\Gamma_{\mathsf{v}}(T)(m), \Gamma_{\mathsf{b}}(T)(m), \mathsf{offset}(addr, T_e)), & \Gamma_{\mathsf{b}}(T)(m) \neq \bot, T \neq \Gamma_{\mathsf{r}}(T)(m) = T_e \in \Gamma_{\mathsf{e}}(T), \\ \mathsf{lookup}(T', \mathsf{ref}(val'), m), & \Gamma_{\mathsf{b}}(T)(m) = \bot, \\ & \quad I \in \Gamma_{\mathsf{i}} \cap \Gamma_{\mathsf{e}}(T), \mathsf{offset}(addr, I) = (T', val'). \end{cases}$$

Fig. 8. Method lookup function of μGo

There's no difference about evaluating the address or value of a variable or field, except that pointers are not in consideration.

$$\sigma, h \vDash \mathsf{ref}(e) = \begin{cases} \sigma(v) & e \text{ is } v, \\ \mathsf{offset}(\sigma(v), a) & e \text{ is } v.a, \end{cases} \qquad \mathsf{eval}(e) = h(\mathsf{ref}(e)).$$

And the dynamic type and reference functions remain the same:

$$\sigma, h \vDash \mathsf{dtype}(e), \mathsf{dref}(e) = \begin{cases} \mathsf{stype}(e), \mathsf{ref}(e), & \mathsf{stype}(e) \notin \Gamma_{\mathsf{i}}, \\ T, \mathsf{offset}(\mathsf{ref}(e), val) & \mathsf{stype}(e) \in \Gamma_{\mathsf{i}}, \text{where } \mathsf{eval}(e) = (T, val). \end{cases}$$

For statements, as in mini-Go, we discuss only the assignment and method invocation. The semantic rules are given in Fig. 7.

As in mini-Go, assigning a non-interface value to an interface variable has different semantics from normal assignment, therefore we also need to define a similar assignment function. However, in μGo, an interface variable preserves the reference of the object with its type, which makes the most significant difference from mini-Go:

$$\sigma, h \vDash \mathsf{assign}(le, e) = \begin{cases} \mathsf{eval}(e), & \mathsf{stype}(le) \notin \Gamma_{\mathsf{i}} \text{ or } \mathsf{stype}(e) \in \Gamma_{\mathsf{i}} \\ (\mathsf{stype}(e), \mathsf{ref}(e)), & \mathsf{stype}(le) \in \Gamma_{\mathsf{i}}, \mathsf{stype}(e) \notin \Gamma_{\mathsf{i}}. \end{cases}$$

Then the rule [μAsn] has the same form of [Asn] in mini-Go, but the semantics of assignment of interface variables is altered.

For method invocations, we define the method lookup function as in mini-Go (Fig. 8). Unlike in mini-Go, the receiver parameter gets a reference rather than a value of the argument while method invocation in μGo. Therefore, the signature of the method lookup function changes to find the local variables, method body and actual receiver reference. Thanks to the absence of pointers, the definition is much simpler.

Having the method body, the method invocation rule [μInv] has the similar form to [Inv] in mini-Go. The most significant difference is that the receiver is now passed by reference, thus the method body and the caller share the same receiver object.

5   Object Model

Mini-Go and μGo give us a solid base to investigate the object model of Go language. In this section we restrict our language facilities in μGo for conciseness, and all the code can be translated to mini-Go/Go without any difficulty.

Go avoid type hierarchy in the language design [5], therefore, there is no class inheritance as in typical OO languages, although the structure types in Go look like classes in C++, and the embedding looks like inheritance. In a glance, embedding in Go works similarly as an inheritance mechanism: all fields and methods from an embedded structure/interface are implicitly taken into the new structure, and a method from an embedded structure or interface will be overridden if a new method with the same signature is defined.

In μGo, it is possible to emulate a real (Java-like) class as follows:

```
type Class interface {
    Method()      }
type ClassImpl struct {
    Field Type    }
func (self ClassImpl) Method() {
    // ...
}
```

```
type SubClass interface {
    Class    // interface inheritance
    Method2()     }
type SubClassImpl struct {
    Class    // implementation inheritance
    Field2 Type2  }
func (self SubClassImpl) Method2() { ... }
```

Where the embedding of interface types are used to support subtyping and polymorphism, and the embedding of structure types are used to support code reusing. Using this program pattern, we can emulate most uses of inheritance, although a little verbose.

However, the structure embedding alone cannot replace class inheritance without help of interface types. Structure embedding does not define a subtype relation. In Go, it is impossible to "downcast" a structure or interface into an embedded structure, and is impossible either even using pointers. And of course it is also impossible to assign a structure to a variable of the embedded structure. This fact shows that the embedding is completely a composition mechanism for code reuse. On the other hand, implementation of interface types is a subtype relation (see Sects. 3.1 and 4.1), and calling a method from an interface variable leads to dynamic dispatch (see Figs. 4 and 8). That's how the code example above works. Therefore, when dynamic dispatch or subtyping is needed, it is necessary to use interface types.

Furthermore, since downcasting is impossible for embedding types, the technique above cannot give full power of OO programming. In Go, method receivers must be explicitly declared. In addition, for a non-interface method, the receiver variable always insist on its static type, but never late-bounds to some subtype of it. This is a special case of lack of downcast that the receiver cannot be cast to its subtype. Therefore, *polymorphism via method receiver is impossible in Go*. In contrast, in typical class-based OO programming languages, e.g. Java, there is a special variable `this` to allow a method in a class to invoke methods that are defined later in a subclass. This late-bound receiver mechanism is called the open recursion feature [6]. And it enables some advanced OO programming techniques.

A good example to demonstrate late-bound receivers is the template design pattern [1]. Supposing we are writing game applications, different games have the same pattern that every portion of a game can be split into several steps. We want to write the procedure only one time for playing the games with different implementations of steps. In C++, the skeleton of the code looks like:

```
class Game { public void play(); public virtual void step(); };
void Game::play() { this->step(); this->step(); }
class ChessGame : public Game { public virtual void step(); /* ... */ };
void ChessGame::step() { /* one step of chess game */ }
int main() { Game *g = new ChessGame(); g->play(); }
```

When invoking `g->play()` in `main`, virtual calls **this**`->step()` are launched, and some real code defined in the subclass, `ChessGame`, is actually executed, although `g` has type `Game`. That is, **this** in `play()` is late and dynamic bounded.

It seems that embedding of structures in μGo is quite similar to the inheritance in C++. An attempt to translate the C++ program to μGo might be:

```
type Game struct {}
func (this Game) Play() {
    this.Step(); this.Step() }   // Error: no Step() method for type Game
type ChessGame struct { Game }
func (this ChessGame) Step() {   /* one step of chess game */ }
func main() {
    var g Game = new(ChessGame)  // Error: ChessGame is not a subtype of Game
    g.Play() }
```

However, this is wrong. Because the structure `Game` does not even know the fact that it is embedded in `ChessGame`, and because the receiver `this` in method `Play()` is not late-bound, it is impossible to call `Step()` method of `ChessGame` type from `Game`'s method. What's more, an object of type `ChessGame` cannot be assigned to variable `g` of type `Game`, because `ChessGame` is not a subtype of `Game`. We see that structure embedding in μGo cannot bring us dynamic dispatch, nor subtyping.

The ordinary way to implement such functionality in Go is to define `Play()` as a (non-method) function which has a `Stepper` parameter, where `Stepper` is an interface with `Step()` method:

```
type Stepper interface { Step() }     func Play(s Stepper) { s.Step(); s.Step() }
```

This is acceptable in simple situations, but different instance types of `Stepper` cannot share the common data fields and methods of games, and there is no proper type to describe the concept of a "game". Thus it is too limited for complicated OO design.

A more sophisticated solution is to define `Game` as a structure for the common fields and methods, and let `Game` embed the `Stepper` interface to support dynamic dispatch:

```
type Stepper interface { Step() }      type Game struct { Stepper }
func (this Game) Play() { this.Step(); this.Step() }
type ChessStepper struct {}
func (this ChessStepper) Step() { /* one step */ }
func main() { var g Game = new(Game); g.Stepper = ChessStepper{}; g.Play() }
```

It is not, however, the *template pattern*, but in fact the *command pattern* [1]. As was pointed out before, embedding is not subtyping. The embedded `Stepper` is not a subtype of `Game`, therefore we cannot access the common fields and methods defined in `Game` from `Step()` method. So this technique is still limited.

We can overcome the limitation by explicitly passing `Game`, the common part of different variants of games, to `Step()` method. Or we can also define a `ChessGame` structure which embeds `Game` and implements `Stepper`, and explicitly pass a `ChessGame` structure as an `ChessStepper` to `Play()` method:

```
type Stepper interface { Step() }      type Game struct { Stepper }
func (this Game) Play(s Stepper) { this.Step(); this.Step() }
type ChessGame struct { Game }
func (this ChessGame) Step() { /* one step */ }
func main() { var g Game = new(ChessGame); g.Play(g) }
```

The so-called client-specified self pattern above is used in [9] to implement template pattern in Go. However, These workarounds are verbose and unnatural that need weird method call like `g.Play(g)`.

Now we propose another solution to explicitly introduce late-bound receivers, which can mimic class-based languages in implementing *template pattern*:

```
type Game interface { Play(); Step() }        func NewChessGame() ChessGame {
type BaseGame struct {                            var g ChessGame = new(ChessGame)
    // explicitly declared late-bound receiver    // bound the dynamic receiver explicitly
    dyn Game  }                                   g.dyn = g
func (g BaseGame) Play() {                         return g  }
    // the late-bound receiver                 func (g ChessGame) Step() { /* one step */ }
    var this Game = g.dyn                      func main() {
    this.Step(); this.Step()  }                   var g Game = NewChessGame()
type ChessGame struct { BaseGame }                g.Play()  }
```

Here `ChessGame` is a subtype of `Chess` since it implements interface `Chess`, and we embed `BaseGame` in `ChessGame` to reuse method `Play()`. In addition, `Play()` could invoke method `Step()` from its super type via `dyn`, so the dynamic dispatch is enabled. The only thing we added is the field `dyn`, which acts a role as the late-bound *this* variable in a class-based OO language. Further, we use the constructor `NewChessGame()` to manually bound `dyn` only once, no wired call like `g.Play(g)` is needed.

Our approach combines the power of embedding structure and interface types. Structure embedding enables code reuse, interface types enable dynamic dispatch and subtyping, and the `dyn` field of an interface type mimics the late-bound receiver. What's more, the `dyn` trick does not affect the use of the method, thus good encapsulation is achieved. This suits the OOP features by Pierce [6] well, and solves the existing problems.

From above discussions, we can conclude that, the absence of late-bound self variable in Go brings an important restriction to combine the powers of dynamic dispatch and code reuse. This absence brings difficulties to invoking a method in the embedded structure, where a dynamic invocation to the method in the embedding structure outside is applied. Although we can use a different design to round about the problem (for example, use the command pattern instead of the template pattern), or we can emulate a class-based language in Go with some extra effort. Neither approach is perfect.

6 Related Work and Conclusions

Since Go is rather young, we have not found model languages like mini-Go and μGo for its OO features been published yet. The idea of duck typing of Go comes from dynamic languages e.g. Python and Ruby, while the interface-based design comes from Java. There are many model languages for investigating the OO features of Java, such as the Featherweight Java [10] and MJ [11]. The idea of separating subtyping and inheritance can be found in Cook et al. [12,13].

Schmager et al. [9] discussed how to implement some design patterns [1] in Go. They pointed out that the template pattern, which is based on type hierarchy, is difficult to implement, and proposed to use client-specified self pattern [14] to overcome the absence of inheritance and late-bound self features. However, their technique is more verbose for programmers and does not support encapsulation well compared to our proposal.

In this paper, we have investigated the OO-related features of Go language, where class inheritance is excluded intensively. Our contributions include:

1. We develop a sequential model language mini-Go of Go language, and build its formal typing rules and structural semantics as a basis of later research.
2. We point out that the pointer types in Go can be dropped without sacrificing Go's expressiveness, and design such a model language μGo with its typing rules and formal semantics.
3. We investigate the OO model of Go using μGo in detail. Go takes a very different object model based on its embedding and interfaces features, which has been proved to be relatively expressive in most situations. But the absence of open recursion brings difficulties to design some programs in Go. And we propose a novel design pattern to mimic the missing feature and overcome the difficulties.

References

1. Gamma, E., Helm, R., Johnson, R., Vlissides, J.: Design Patterns: Elements of Reusable Object-oriented Software. Pearson Education, Upper Saddle River (1994)
2. Tempero, E., Boyland, J., Melton, H.: How do Java programs use inheritance? an empirical study of inheritance in Java software. In: Vitek, J. (ed.) ECOOP 2008. LNCS, vol. 5142, pp. 667–691. Springer, Heidelberg (2008)

3. The Go Authors: The Go Programming Language Specification, 1.4.2 edn., November 2014
4. Pike, R.: Go at Google: Language design in the service of software engineering
5. The Go Authors: The Go Programming Language: FAQ, 1.4.2 edn., November 2014
6. Pierce, B.C.: Types and Programming Languages. MIT Press, Cambridge (2002)
7. Liu, H., Qiu, Z.: Go model and object oriented programming. Technical report, School of Mathematical Science, Peking University (2015)
8. Plotkin, G.D.: A structural approach to operational semantics. J. Log. Algebraic Program. **60–61**, 17–139 (2004)
9. Schmager, F., Cameron, N., Noble, J.: GoHotDraw: evaluating the Go programming language with design patterns. In: Evaluation and Usability of Programming Languages and Tools, p. 10. ACM (2010)
10. Igarashi, A., Pierce, B.C., Wadler, P.: Featherweight Java: a minimal core calculus for Java and GJ. ACM Trans. Program. Lang. Syst. **23**(3), 396–450 (2001)
11. Bierman, G.M., Parkinson, M.J., Pitts, A.M.: MJ: an imperative core calculus for Java and Java with effects. Technical report 563, University of Cambridge Computer Laboratory, April 2003
12. Cook, W.R., Hill, W., Canning, P.S.: Inheritance is not subtyping. In: Proceedings of the 17th ACM SIGPLAN-SIGACT Symposium on Principles of Programming Languages, POPL 1990, pp. 125–135. ACM, New York (1990)
13. Cook, W.R.: On understanding data abstraction, revisited. SIGPLAN Not. **44**(10), 557–572 (2009)
14. Viljamaa, P.: Client-specified self. In: Pattern Languages Of Program Design, pp. 495–504. ACM Press/Addison-Wesley Publishing Co., New York (1995)

An Intrinsic Denotational Semantics for a Lazy Functional Language

Leonardo Rodríguez[✉]

FaMAF, Universidad Nacional de Córdoba, Córdoba, Argentina
lrodrig2@famaf.unc.edu.ar

Abstract. In this paper we present a denotational semantics for a lazy functional language. The semantics is intrinsic in the sense that it defines meaning for typing derivations instead of language expressions. We contrast our semantics with the well-known evaluation rules defined by Sestoft [17] and show that these rules preserve types and meaning.

Keywords: Denotational semantics · Lazy evaluation · Type theory

1 Introduction

In a lazy functional language, function arguments are evaluated only if needed and at most once. The evaluation is performed in normal order and with *sharing* of arguments evaluation. This paper presents a denotational semantics for a lazy language that models this evaluation strategy. The semantics is *intrinsic* in the sense of Reynolds [15, 16], since it defines meaning to typing judgements rather than to terms themselves, and as a consequence, only well-typed terms have meaning.

The semantics of lazy languages have been largely studied, and there are many operational specifications and abstract machines based on graph reduction [8, 10], super-combinators [7], and other techniques. Launchbury [12] defined a big-step operational semantics for an extended lambda calculus. The sharing of evaluation is modelled using *heaps* mapping variables to its values, which are updated when the evaluation of an expression is finished. Sestoft [17] revised the semantics by providing a way to locally check freshness of variables during evaluation, among others improvements. This paper takes the same language used by Sestoft but with the inclusion of a type-system. We define an intrinsic denotational semantics for the language, and show that the evaluation rules preserve both types and meaning.

There are other denotational definitions of the semantics for lazy functional languages [3, 4, 9]. Launchbury [12] defined a denotational semantics and presented a proof of adequacy with respect to his evaluation rules. However, Breitner [6] have recently found some issues in the proof, and then adjusted the semantics to correct them. Nakata [13] presented an alternative definition to the denotational semantics for recursive local declarations. In [13], like in this paper, a type system is included in the language, but its semantic definition is nonetheless untyped.

© Springer International Publishing Switzerland 2015
A. Pardo and S.D. Swierstra (Eds.): SBLP 2015, LNCS 9325, pp. 75–80, 2015.
DOI: 10.1007/978-3-319-24012-1_6

2   Syntax and Semantics

We use the same language as in [12,17], a lambda calculus with recursive local declarations which presents terms in a restricted syntax:

Definition 1 (Language terms)
$$e ::= \lambda x.\, e \mid e\, x \mid x \mid let\, \{x_i \mapsto e_i\}\, in\, e$$

The purpose of this restricted form is to ensure that every function argument has been previously bound by a local declaration (*let*), and therefore it will be shared in the heap, as will become clear later. Note that a general lambda expression may be translated into this restricted syntax by introducing new let-bindings.

Notation: Before we continue let us fix some notations about finite maps (used to represent heaps, contexts and environments). Let $M : D \to R$ be a finite map from a set D (the domain of M) to some set R (the range of M). We write $M[x \mapsto r]$ for the extension of M with a new map $\{x \mapsto r\}$. Sometimes we write $M[x_i \mapsto r_i]$ as a shortening of $M[x_1 \mapsto r_1] \ldots [r_n \mapsto r_n]$, and if $D_0 \subseteq D$ we write $M|_{D_0}$ for the restriction of M to the domain D_0. Finally, if M and M' are maps with disjoint domain, we write $M \sqcup M'$ for the combination of the two maps in a single one.

Figure 1 shows Sestoft's evaluation rules. A heap Γ is a finite map from variables to expressions, and a pair of the form (Γ, e) where e is an expression is called a configuration. A judgement of the form $(\Gamma, e) \Downarrow_A (\Delta, w)$ says that in the heap Γ, the expression e will evaluate to w producing a new heap Δ.

The evaluation rules are annotated with a set A of the variables whose value is being computed at the time. The only place where this set is updated is in the VAR rule when the value of x is about to be computed.

The rule VAR is where sharing becomes evident. Once the expression e is evaluated, the variable x is updated in heap Δ with its new value w, avoiding in this way to evaluate the variable x again in the future.

In the LET rule we write $\hat{e}$ for the substitution $e[z_1 \backslash x_1, \ldots, z_n \backslash x_n]$. The variables z_i have to be fresh: they must not occur in Γ, A or $let\, \{x_i \mapsto e_i\}\, in\, e$.

$$\text{ABST} \frac{}{(\Gamma, \lambda x.\, e) \Downarrow_A (\Gamma, \lambda x.\, e)} \qquad \text{VAR} \frac{(\Gamma, e) \Downarrow_{A \cup \{x\}} (\Delta, w)}{(\Gamma[x \mapsto e], x) \Downarrow_A (\Delta[x \mapsto w], w)}$$

$$\text{APP} \frac{(\Gamma, e) \Downarrow_A (\Delta, \lambda y.\, e') \qquad (\Delta, e'[x \backslash y]) \Downarrow_A (\Theta, w)}{(\Gamma, e\, x) \Downarrow_A (\Theta, w)}$$

$$\text{LET} \frac{(\Gamma[z_i \mapsto \hat{e}_i], \hat{e}) \Downarrow_A (\Delta, w)}{(\Gamma, let\, \{x_i \mapsto e_i\}\, in\, e) \Downarrow_A (\Delta, w)}$$

Fig. 1. Big-step operational semantics

Notice that, unlike in [12], the checking of freshness can be done locally (that is, looking only at the configuration being evaluated and not at the entire evaluation tree).

It is necessary to ensure that the substitution $e'[x\backslash y]$ does not capture the variable x (in the APP rule), and also that the variable x does not occur in the domain of Δ (in the VAR rule), and hence the extension $\Delta[x \mapsto w]$ does not overwrite any map of Δ. In order to guarantee those properties it is required for the evaluation to produce only "A-good" configurations, as defined in [17]. For convenience we reproduce the definition here:

Definition 2. *A configuration (Γ, e) is A-good if and only if*
1. $A \cap dom(\Gamma) = \emptyset$, 2. $Fv(\Gamma, e) \subseteq A \cup dom(\Gamma)$, 3. $Bv(\Gamma, e) \cap (A \cup dom(\Gamma)) = \emptyset$.

Here $Fv(\Gamma, e)$ denotes the set of free variables of the entire configuration, including the expressions in the range of Γ. Similarly, the set $Bv(\Gamma, e)$ contains all the bound variables of the configuration (Γ, e). The following lemma, proved in [17], shows that indeed "A-good" is preserved by evaluation.

Lemma 1. *If (Γ, e) is A-good and $(\Gamma, e) \Downarrow_A (\Delta, w)$ is derivable, then (Δ, w) is A-good and $dom(\Gamma) \subseteq dom(\Delta)$.*

3   Type System

In Fig. 2, we define the typing rules for expressions, heaps and configurations.

A typing judgment for an expression e has the usual form $\pi \vdash e : \theta$, where π is a context and θ is a type. We have two type constructors, the basic type b and arrow types of the form $\theta \rightarrow \theta'$. Contexts are finite maps from variables to types.

On the other hand, a typing judgement for a heap Γ has the form $\pi' \vdash \Gamma : \pi$, where both π' and π are contexts. The first context π' is necessary since a heap may contain free variables: in the Var evaluation rule, the variable x may occur

$$
\text{TyAbs} \dfrac{\pi[x \mapsto \theta] \vdash e : \theta'}{\pi \vdash \lambda x.\, e : \theta \rightarrow \theta'} \qquad \text{TyApp} \dfrac{\pi \vdash e : \theta \rightarrow \theta' \quad \{x \mapsto \theta\} \in \pi}{\pi \vdash e\, x : \theta'}
$$

$$
\text{TyVar} \dfrac{\{x \mapsto \theta\} \in \pi}{\pi \vdash x : \theta} \qquad \text{TyLet} \dfrac{\pi[x_i \mapsto \theta_i] \vdash e_i : \theta_i \quad \pi[x_i \mapsto \theta_i] \vdash e : \theta'}{\pi \vdash let\, \{x_i \mapsto e_i\}\, in\, e : \theta'}
$$

$$
\text{TyEmpty} \dfrac{}{\pi' \vdash \diamond : []} \qquad \text{TyExt} \dfrac{\pi'[x \mapsto \theta] \vdash \Gamma : \pi \quad \pi' \sqcup \pi[x \mapsto \theta] \vdash e : \theta}{\pi' \vdash \Gamma[x \mapsto e] : \pi[x \mapsto \theta]}
$$

$$
\text{TyConf} \dfrac{\pi' \vdash \Gamma : \pi \quad \pi' \sqcup \pi \vdash e : \theta}{(\pi', \pi) \vdash (\Gamma, e) : \theta}
$$

Fig. 2. Typing rules

free in the range of the heap and still be removed from its domain and included in the set A. Thus, the context π' is intended to type each variable in A, whereas the context π is meant to type each variable in the domain of Γ.

We have a single rule to type a configuration (Γ, e) that combines a typing derivation for the heap Γ and a typing derivation for the expression e. Note that the use of the operation $\pi' \sqcup \pi$ has the implicit requirement for the domain of π' and π to be disjoint. This is ensured if the configuration (Γ, e) is $dom(\pi')$-good. The following lemma states that the evaluation rules preserves types:

Lemma 2 (Type preservation). *Let (Γ, e) and (Δ, w) be configurations, π' and π_0 contexts, and θ a type such that:*

1. (Γ, e) is $dom(\pi')$-good, 2. $(\pi', \pi_0) \vdash (\Gamma, e) : \theta$, 3. $(\Gamma, e) \Downarrow_{dom(\pi')} (\Delta, w)$.

Then, there is a context π_1 such that $\pi_0 \subseteq \pi_1$ and $(\pi', \pi_1) \vdash (\Delta, w) : \theta$.

Proof. The proof is by structural induction on the evaluation rules. In each case, it is necessary to perform inversion in the typing derivation and to use Lemma 1.

4   Denotational Semantics

We used a domain-theoretic setting to define the semantics of the language. The meaning of a type θ is a domain $[\![\theta]\!]$ and the meaning of a context π is an environment $[\![\pi]\!]$ (a named finite product ordered pointwise).

In Fig. 3 we present some of the equations of the semantics. We define three functions $\mathcal{E}[\![\_]\!]_{\pi, \theta}$, $\mathcal{H}[\![\_]\!]_{\pi, \pi'}$ and $\mathcal{C}[\![\_]\!]_{\pi', \theta}$ that assign a continuous function to a typing derivation for a expression, a heap and a configuration, respectively.

It can be proved that this semantics is *coherent*: different typing derivations with the same conclusion have the same meaning. This property allow us to write without ambiguity $\mathcal{E}[\![e]\!]_{\pi, \theta}$ for the semantics of any typing derivation with conclusion $\pi \vdash e : \theta$ (and the same holds for the other forms of judgement). We refer to [14] for a proof of coherence of the semantics for a language larger than the one we use in this paper.

Notation: Let us clarify some notation we use in Fig. 3. The symbol $\hat{\lambda}$ is used as a meta-binder to avoid confusion with the symbol λ used in abstractions. If η is an environment, we write $\eta \,/\, x$ for its projection on the variable x. Finally, we write $\mathbf{Y}_D\, f$ for the least fixed-point of a continuous function $f : D \to D$ where D is a domain.

The following lemma says that evaluation rules preserve meaning. This lemma corresponds to "Theorem 2" in [12] (correctness of denotational semantics), but this time proved for the revised semantics of Sestoft and including only well-typed configurations.

$$\mathcal{E}[\![\,_-\,]\!]_{\pi,\theta} : [\![\,\pi\,]\!] \to [\![\,\theta\,]\!]$$

$$\mathcal{E}[\![\,\lambda x.\,e\,]\!]_{\pi,\theta\to\theta'}\,\eta = \hat\lambda d.\;\mathcal{E}[\![\,e\,]\!]_{\pi[x\mapsto\theta],\theta'}\,(\eta[x\mapsto d])$$

$$\mathcal{E}[\![\,e\,x\,]\!]_{\pi,\theta'}\,\eta = \mathcal{E}[\![\,e\,]\!]_{\pi,\theta\to\theta'}\,\eta\,(\mathcal{E}[\![\,x\,]\!]_{\pi,\theta}\,\eta)$$

$$\mathcal{E}[\![\,x\,]\!]_{\pi,\theta}\,\eta = \eta\downarrow x$$

$$\mathcal{E}[\![\,let\,\{x_i\mapsto e_i\}\,in\,e\,]\!]_{\pi,\theta}\,\eta = \mathcal{E}[\![\,e\,]\!]_{\pi[x_i\mapsto\theta_i],\theta}\,\eta'$$

$$\eta' = \mathbf{Y}_{\pi[x_i\mapsto\theta_i]}\,(\hat\lambda\eta'.\;\eta[x_i\mapsto\mathcal{E}[\![\,e_i\,]\!]_{\pi[x_i\mapsto\theta_i],\theta_i}\,\eta'])$$

$$\mathcal{H}[\![\,_-\,]\!]_{\pi',\pi} : [\![\,\pi'\,]\!] \to [\![\,\pi\,]\!]$$

$$\mathcal{H}[\![\,\diamond\,]\!]_{\pi',[]}\,\eta = ()$$

$$\mathcal{H}[\![\,\Gamma[x\mapsto e]\,]\!]_{\pi',\pi[x\mapsto\theta]}\,\eta = \mathbf{Y}_{[\![\,\pi[x\mapsto\theta]\,]\!]}\,(\hat\lambda\eta'.\;\eta''[x\mapsto d])$$

$$\text{where } d = \mathcal{E}[\![\,e\,]\!]_{\pi'\sqcup\pi[x\mapsto\theta],\theta}\,(\eta\sqcup\eta')$$

$$\eta'' = \mathcal{H}[\![\,\Gamma\,]\!]_{\pi'[x\mapsto\theta],\pi}\,(\eta[x\mapsto d])$$

$$\mathcal{C}[\![\,_-\,]\!]_{\pi',\theta} : [\![\,\pi'\,]\!] \to [\![\,\theta\,]\!]$$

$$\mathcal{C}[\![\,(\Gamma,e)\,]\!]_{\pi',\theta}\,\eta = \mathcal{E}[\![\,e\,]\!]_{\pi'||\pi,\theta}\,(\eta\sqcup\mathcal{H}[\![\,\Gamma\,]\!]_{\pi',\pi}\,\eta)$$

Fig. 3. Denotational semantics.

Lemma 3 (Semantic preservation). *Let (Γ, e) and (Δ, w) be configurations, π', π_0, π_1 be contexts, and θ a type such that,*

1. $(\pi', \pi_0) \vdash (\Gamma, e) : \theta,$ 3. $\pi_0 \subseteq \pi_1,$
2. (Γ, e) is $dom(\pi')$-good,   4. $(\pi', \pi_1) \vdash (\Delta, w) : \theta.$

Then, if $(\Gamma, e) \Downarrow_{dom(\pi')} (\Delta, w)$, for all $\eta \in [\![\,\pi'\,]\!]$ it holds:
1. $\mathcal{C}[\![\,(\Gamma, e)\,]\!]_{\pi',\theta}\,\eta = \mathcal{C}[\![\,(\Delta, w)\,]\!]_{\pi',\theta}\,\eta,$ 2. $\mathcal{H}[\![\,\Gamma\,]\!]_{\pi',\pi_0}\,\eta = (\mathcal{H}[\![\,\Delta\,]\!]_{\pi',\pi_1}\,\eta)|_{dom(\pi_0)}.$

Proof. The proof is by structural induction on the evaluation rules. It is necessary to use Lemma 2 to construct the typing derivations required to apply inductive hypothesis in each case.

The complete proof of this lemma is longer than the untyped version presented in [12], but each step in the proof is type-driven and has the simplicity provided by the typed framework.

5 Further Work

We have not yet proved computational adequacy of the semantics in the sense of [12, Sect. 5]. For instance, we should prove that if the semantics of a term is non-bottom, then the term evaluates to a normal form.

Our goal behind this intrinsic definition of the semantics is to prove the correctness of Sestoft's abstract machine [17] using type-indexed logical relations.

In our experience, intrinsic semantics are more suitable for formalization in a proof assistant with dependent types since all the semantic functions are total (without the need of type-error constants that usually complicate the semantic equations). We expect to formalize the results in this work using the Coq [2] proof assistant together with a domain theory library developed by Benton et al. [5]. We extended this library and used it to a formalize a denotational semantics for a call-by-name functional language, and a proof of correctness for a compiler targeting the Krivine abstract machine [11]. Our development is available online [1].

References

1. Some Formalizations in Coq. http://cs.famaf.unc.edu.ar/leorodriguez/compiler correctness/
2. The Coq Proof Assistant. http://coq.inria.fr/
3. Abramsky, S.: The lazy lambda calculus. In: Turner, D. (ed.) Research Topics in Functional Programming, pp. 65–116. Addison-Wesley, Boston (1990)
4. Abramsky, S., Ong, C.L.: Full abstraction in the lazy lambda calculus. Inf. Comput. **105**(2), 159–267 (1993)
5. Benton, N., Kennedy, A., Varming, C.: Formalizing Domains, Ultrametric Spaces and Semantics of Programming Languages (2010), unpublished
6. Breitner, J.: The correctness of Launchbury's natural semantics for lazy evaluation. Archive of Formal Proofs (2013)
7. Hughes, R.J.M.: Super-combinators: a new implementation method for applicative languages. In: Proceedings of the 1982 ACM Symposium on LISP and Functional Programming, LFP 1982, pp. 1–10. ACM, New York (1982)
8. Jones, P.L.S.: Implementing lazy functional languages on stock hardware: the spineless tagless G-machine. J. Funct. Program. **2**(2), 127–202 (1992)
9. Josephs, M.B.: The semantics of lazy functional languages. Theor. Compu. Sci. **68**(1), 105–111 (1989)
10. Kieburtz, R.B.: The G-machine: a fast, graph-reduction evaluator. In: Jouannaud, J.P. (ed.) FPLCA 1985. LNCS, vol. 201, pp. 400–413. Springer, Heidelberg (1985)
11. Krivine, J.L.: A call-by-name lambda-calculus machine. High. Order Symbolic Comput. **20**(3), 199–207 (2007)
12. Launchbury, J.: A natural semantics for lazy evaluation. In: POPL, pp. 144–154 (1993)
13. Nakata, K.: Denotational semantics for lazy initialization of letrec: black holes as exceptions rather than divergence. In: 7th Workshop on Fixed Points in Computer Science (2010)
14. Reynolds, J.C.: The Coherence of Languages with Intersection Types. In: Ito, T., Meyer, A.R. (eds.) TACS 1991. LNCS, vol. 526, pp. 675–700. Springer, Heidelberg (1991)
15. Reynolds, J.C.: Theories of Programming Languages. Cambridge University Press, New York (1999)
16. Reynolds, J.C.: The Meaning of Types - From Intrinsic to Extrinsic Semantics. Technical report RS-00-32, BRICS, December 2000
17. Sestoft, P.: Deriving a lazy abstract machine. J. Funct. Program. **7**(3), 231–264 (1997)

Color Flipping

Felipe L. Silva[✉], Marcelo F. Luna, and Wesley Attrot

State University of Londrina, Londrina, Brazil
{felipe.lds.88,marcelofernandesdeluna}@gmail.com
wesley@uel.br

Abstract. Spill code minimization is an important problem in register allocation because it affects the quality of the code produced by the compiler and program performance. This work presents a new technique to reduce spill code, called color flipping. Differently of other techniques, color flipping prevents all load/store instructions insertion when avoiding spill. Nevertheless, color flipping can be used in combination with other spill minimization techniques to achieve an overall better result. To evaluate the impact of using color flipping, experiments with a set of interference graphs and with the benchmark SPEC CPU2006, showed over 12 % of spill reduction.

Keywords: Spill minimization · Register allocation · Color flipping

1 Introduction

Register allocation [10, 16, 18, 23] is one of the most important compiler optimizations. It directly affects the quality of the code produced. The goal of register allocation is to keep as many as possible temporary values created by a program in machine registers. The problem in register allocation occurs when the finite number of available machine registers can not fit the unbounded temporary values. When this occurs some values must be kept in memory, which decreases the speed of the generated code. To keep the temporaries in memory, load/store instructions are inserted into the code; this process is called spill code generation.

The most widely used algorithm to perform register allocation is graph coloring [7,10,15]. In this approach, the compiler builds an interference graph G, where each node represents a live range and edges connecting two live ranges l_i and l_j symbolizes an interference and means that l_i and l_j will be live at the same time in the future and should not occupy the same register. The problem then is to find a proper K-coloring for G, such that no two adjacent nodes receive the same color. By representing the colors as machine registers we can perform register allocation with a coloring algorithm.

An ideal register allocator should produce the minimum amount of spill code possible to avoid unnecessary memory accesses, and therefore slowdown the executable code. However, introducing the minimum spill code as possible is an NP-complete problem.

© Springer International Publishing Switzerland 2015
A. Pardo and S.D. Swierstra (Eds.): SBLP 2015, LNCS 9325, pp. 81–95, 2015.
DOI: 10.1007/978-3-319-24012-1_7

Several efforts have been made to find efficient techniques to reduce the impact of spills in the code. In 1989 Bernstein *et al.* [5] improved the Chaitin's allocator with new heuristics to select the spill node known as *best-of-three*. In the same year, Briggs *et al.* [6] developed a stronger coloring heuristic, called *optimistic coloring*. In 1992 Briggs *et al.* [8] also extended the *rematerialization* notion of Chaitin by dealing with multi-valued live ranges. The rematerialization recomputes constant values when it is cheaper than to store and reload it. In 1997 Bergner *et al.* [4] developed a new minimization technique, known as *interference region spilling* that was able to spill partially a live range. Later in 1998, Cooper and Simpson [13] developed a new technique to globally split live ranges similar to that developed by Bergner *et al.* [4] known as *live range splitting*. In 2003, Govindarajan *et al.* [17] developed a heuristic to reduce the numbers of registers used by instruction sequencing, called *Minimum Register Instruction Sequence (MRIS)*. In the same year, Koseki *et al.* [20] developed a new technique for partial spilling called *spill code motion*. In 2005, Gao and Shi [14] created a method, named *merge* that allows two interfered nodes in the interference graph occupy the same machine register. Finally in 2013, Barany and Krall [3] developed a *global code motion* to order basic blocks with the aim of reduce overlaps among live ranges.

The majority of previous spill code minimization research efforts have been focused on studying spilling heuristics to select the live range with the smallest spill cost [5,9] and finer spilling/splitting mechanisms to reduce the number of load/store instructions inserted [4,7,13]. Unlike these techniques we introduce a technique called *color flipping* which focuses on the coloring stage of graph coloring algorithm, where if *color flipping* succeeds no load/store instructions are inserted because a register is assigned for the entire live range. The main idea is to attempt to recolor [19] the interference graph, such that a used color becomes available for spill node.

2   Color Flipping

To demonstrate how *color flipping* works, we present a simple example where the spill is successfully avoided. The interference graph and its corresponding node costs are shown in Fig. 1. In this example, we will assume that we have 3 colors available, that is, $K = 3$.

After coloring the interference graph, we are left with the 3-colored sub-graph shown in Fig. 2(a) and the uncolored live range F. Normally we would spill the live range F. However, observing this graph we notice that F has three neighbors with unique colors: $A : green$, $B : blue$ and $E : red$. So, if we change the color of any of these nodes, then we will make a color available for F. By extending this idea to one more level of the interference graph, i.e., searching for nodes with unique color in the neighborhood of A, B and E, we can start to flip colors. Analyzing the neighbors of A, we find that A has no neighbor with unique color, so we proceed our analysis to B. We observe that B has one neighbor with unique color, that is, $A : green$, $C : green$ and $D : red$. As B is the only *blue*

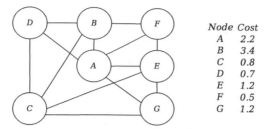

Fig. 1. Interference graph and its spill costs.

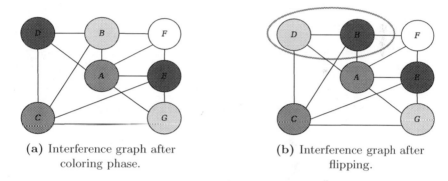

(a) Interference graph after coloring phase.

(b) Interference graph after flipping.

Fig. 2. Flipping colors in the graph (Color figure online).

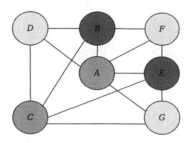

Fig. 3. Final result after applying color flipping in Fig. 2(a) and continuing register allocation (Color figure online).

node connected to D, so, it's possible to flip B and D colors, as seen in Fig. 2(b). Now we are free to color F with *blue* as shown in Fig. 3.

In Fig. 2(a) we flipped colors between two neighboring nodes. But it is also possible to recolor a node if it has another color available. In the next example we present a situation where recolor a node in this way makes a color available for the spill node. The interference graph after the coloring phase and after color flipping is shown in Fig. 4. We assume that $K = 4$. There are two physical registers $R1$ and $R3$ already in the graph. Node F interferes with $R1$; nodes

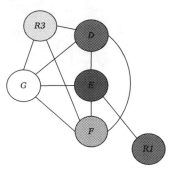

(a) Interference graph after coloring phase.

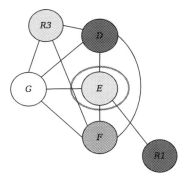

(b) Interference graph after flipping.

Fig. 4. Flipping colors in the graph (Color figure online).

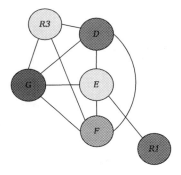

Fig. 5. Final result after applying color flipping in Fig. 4(a) and continuing register allocation (Color figure online).

D, F and G interfere with $R3$. There is no color available for live range G. By observing this graph, we notice that E has another color available, because it can be recolored with *yellow*. Recoloring E in this way, makes *red* available for G. The Fig. 5 shows the result after applying color flipping in the graph.

The main advantage of color flipping over other spill minimization techniques is that when avoiding a live range spill, no load/store instructions are inserted. The color flipping avoids completely the spill, not only partially.

3   Color Flipping Algorithm

To implement color flipping we added an additional stage after the coloring phase. This stage attempts to assign a register for each spilled live range. If color flipping succeeds the live range is removed from the spill list and added to the colored nodes list, otherwise no modification is made on the interference

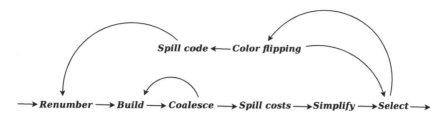

Fig. 6. Color flipping added to Briggs' allocator.

graph and the live range is spilled. The Fig. 6 shows the Briggs' allocator [7] with color flipping stage added.

Given an interference graph G, and a spill node $s \in G$ the color flipping algorithm tries to recolor G such that a valid register R is made available for s. To do so we divided color flipping into two modules: FindFlippingCandidates and TryFlipping.

The aim of the first module is to find a set of *flipping candidates*, i.e., nodes that may have their colors flipped. It begins analyzing each neighbor n_i of the spill nodes to determine if n_i satisfies three constraints called **flipping restrictions**. A list - flippingCandidates - containing the neighbors that meet all flipping restrictions is created.

Once the first module has finished the algorithm starts TryFlipping. In this module each flipping candidate $f_i \in$ flippingCandidates is analyzed to determine if f_i satisfies one of two **flipping conditions**. In positive case f_i is recolored, such that, a color is made available to the spill node and the algorithm stops. Otherwise the *color flipping* algorithm calls FindFlippingCandidates but with I and f_i (not s) as input. This process is repeated until there is no more flipping candidates, that is, flippingCandidates $= \emptyset$. We can stop TryFlipping before setting a max level of recursion - maxLevel - such that *color flipping* stops trying to find new flipping candidate when maxLevel is reached. Figure 7 shows a simple flowchart of TryFlipping.

The flipping restrictions and the flipping conditions are constraints imposed to a node n_i to guarantee that is safe to flip n_i color. By safe, we mean that all constraints of the interference graph after *color flipping* are preserved. When n_i satisfies all flipping restrictions, then n_i is a *potential* flip node. The next step is to analyze n_i to determine if n_i is an *actual* flipping node, that is, determine if n_i satisfies one flipping condition. In order to understand how the *color flipping* algorithm works, one needs a deeper understanding of the criteria used in flipping restrictions and those used in flipping conditions.

Flipping Restrictions: The FindFlippingCandidates module is responsible for finding nodes that satisfy the three flipping restrictions. The input is a node in the interference graph, which we call the target node T, and the output is a list of nodes that meets all three restrictions, which we call flippingCandidates.

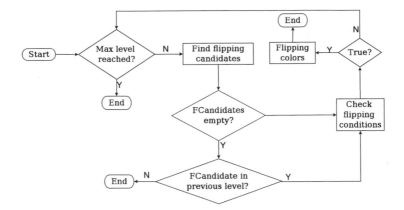

Fig. 7. Flowchart of `TryFlipping` module.

- *First flipping restriction*: this restriction must ensure that the flipping candidate has a unique color among the neighbors of the target node. In Fig. 8(a), T contains three neighbors of the same color. Therefore X, Y and Z do not satisfy the first flipping restriction. In Fig. 8(b) Z satisfies the first flipping restriction. With this restriction we guarantee that if a flipping candidate change its color, then T is free to receive its old color. For our example, in Fig. 8(b) if Z is recolored, we are free to color T with *green*.

- *Second flipping restriction*: this restriction ensures that the flipping candidate is colored with a proper register R_i for T. By proper register we mean that R_i does not interferes with T. In the sub-graph of Fig. 9 the node Z is the unique among the neighbors of the target node T colored with *blue*. However, $R1$ interferes with T, which makes Z to violate the second restriction. If we remove $R1$ from the interference graph, then Z satisfies the second flipping restriction.

- *Third flipping restriction*: we say that `FindFlippingCandidates` is on the first level of an interference graph if T is a spill node. If T has flipping candidates, then each one of them may be target nodes, if so we say that we are at level > 1 of the interference graph. Once `FindFlippingCandidates` begins to operate at a level > 1 of the interference graph, the third flipping restriction is triggered. Otherwise this restriction is always satisfied. Consider the graph in Fig. 10, when we begin searching for flipping candidates of T, we find that W satisfies the first and the second flipping restrictions. As we are in the first level, it's unnecessary to check the third flipping restriction, so W is a flipping candidate of T. The algorithm proceeds to determine the flipping candidates of W and finds that Z satisfies the first and second the flipping restrictions. But Z is neighbor of T violating the third flipping restriction.

  So the aim of the third flipping restriction is ensure that a flipping candidate does not interfere with a target node of the previous flipping candidate. In the example of Fig. 10, it must ensure that the flipping candidates of the

Algorithm 1. Finds flipping candidates

```
1: procedure FINDFLIPCANDIDATES(T)
2:     for all i ∈ T.Adjs do
3:         if i.color ∈ T.PreColored then
4:             continue
5:         for all j ∈ T.Adjs − {i} do
6:             if !(i.color = j.color) then
7:                 continue
8:             if !(T.ancestor ∉ i.Adjs) then
9:                 continue
10:            i.ancestor ← T
11:            flippingCandidates.insert(i)
12:    return flippingCandidates
```

target node W do not interfere with T. If we remove the interference between Z and T, then Z becomes a flipping candidate of W.

The Algorithm 1 shows the implementation of FindFlippingCandidates. The line 2 checks if i satisfies the second flipping restriction, line 6 checks if i satisfies the first flipping restriction, finally line 8 checks if i satisfies the third flipping restriction. If i meets all flipping restrictions, then it's added to the list of flipping candidates on line 11.

(a) First restriction unsatisfied.

(b) First restriction satisfied.

Fig. 8. First flipping restriction example (Color figure online).

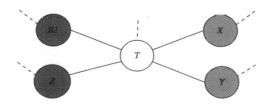

Fig. 9. Second flipping restriction unsatisfied (Color figure online).

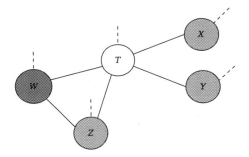

Fig. 10. Third flipping restriction unsatisfied.

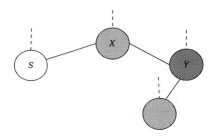

Fig. 11. An interference graph where the second flipping condition fails (Color figure online).

Flipping Conditions: The `TryFlipping` module is responsible for finding nodes that satisfy one of two flipping conditions. The input is a spill node in the interference graph and the desired level of recursion. The output is a valid color for the spill node if color flipping succeeds or -1 if color flipping fails.

- *First flipping condition*: The first flipping condition deals with abusive using of colors that pre-colored nodes may lead in the interference graph. The Fig. 4(a) shows an example of interference graph, which satisfies the first flipping condition. After the coloring phase, it is found that G is a spill node. So we triggered the color flipping algorithm and we found that D, E and F are marked nodes of G. Since E can also be colored with *yellow*, the color *red* is made available for G.
- *Second flipping condition*: The second flipping condition operates at least in three nodes. So it is only triggered from a recursion level > 1. For example, consider the interference graph fragment shown in Fig. 11, if S is a spill node, X a flipping candidate of S, and Y flipping candidate of X, the second flipping condition must ensure that Y has no neighbor with the same color of X. In Fig. 11 flipping the colors of X and Y will not be possible because Y has a neighbor colored with *green*.

An implementation of `TryFlipping` is shown in Algorithm 2. The line 2 checks if the max level of recursion was reached and stops the algorithm in

Algorithm 2. Tries to flipping some nodes colors

```
 1: procedure TRYFLIPPING(UPNODE, LEVEL)
 2:     if level = 0 then
 3:         return -1
 4:     FlipCandidates ← FindFlipCandidates(upNode)
 5:     if FlipCandidates.size() = 0 then
 6:         return -1
 7:     for all i ∈ FlipCandidates do
 8:         if i.allowed.size() > 0 then
 9:             flipColor ← i.color
10:             i.color ← i.allowed.next()
11:             return flipColor
12:         else if upNode.color ≠ −1 then
13:             IAdjs ← AdjList(i) − upNode
14:             if upNode.color ∉ IAdjs.colors then
15:                 flipColor ← i.color
16:                 i.color ← upNode.color
17:                 return flipColor
18:         else if level > 0 then
19:             downFlipColor ← TryFlippingColor(i, level − 1)
20:             if downflipColor > −1 then
21:                 upFlipColor ← i.color
22:                 i.color ← downFlipColor
23:                 return upFlipColor
24:     return -1
```

positive case. The line 4 calls the module `FindFlippingCandidates` and stores its results in `FlipCandidates`. Lines 7–23 loop through each element of the list `FlipCandidates`, to determine if one of them satisfies one of the flipping conditions. Lines 8–11 check the first flipping condition and lines 12–17 check the second flipping condition.

Complexity: The most costing operation in color flipping algorithm is the computation of the first restriction. Given an interference graph G with n nodes, the first restriction needs $(n-1)(n-2)$ comparisons in the worst case, i.e., the cost is $O(n^2)$. Where $(n-1)$ is the number of nodes in G less the spill node and $(n-2)$ is the number of nodes in G less the spill node and the node that is under evaluation in the first restriction. On the other hand, in the best case it's not necessary to compute the first restriction, because the algorithm stops in the second restriction analysis. The number of comparisons to calculate the second flipping restriction is bounded by the number of registers in the target machine. If we represent the number of registers as c, the second restriction needs $c(n-1)$ comparisons to be computed, which gives to color flipping a cost of $\Omega(n)$ in the best case. Based in some of our experimental analysis of color flipping execution, we noticed that the second restriction occurs with considerable frequency, which makes color flipping cost similar to the best case.

4   Experimental Results and Discussion

There are many reasonable ways to measure the quality of a good register allocator - compile time, space requirements, produced executable code efficiency. The main objective of color flipping is to improve code efficiency of allocators that use graph coloring approach. Although an additional cost of space and time is introduced when the color flipping is added to the framework of these allocators, the trend is not to cause severe damage in the performance, since it operates on very limited portions of the graph. This section presents a series of comparisons to measure the impact on the quality of the code when the color flipping is added to Briggs' allocator [7].

To evaluate the efficiency of color flipping two main experiments have been made. The first one takes a set of $27,921$ interference graphs made available by Appel and George [2] to measure how many live range spills were possible to avoid using the color flipping technique. The second experiment, implements the Briggs' allocator with color flipping stage added in LLVM framework [21]. Several comparisons were made between the existing allocators of LLVM. The tests were performed in a Core i5 machine, with 8 GB of RAM in Ubuntu 14.04 64 bits.

4.1   Appel and George Graph Experiments

The set of graphs available by Appel and George [2] were generated from the self-compilation of SML/JN (Standard ML of New Jersey) [1] - a compiler for the language Standard ML '97 - to test new allocation techniques for graph coloring, without relying on any specific framework.

The samples assume that $K = 21$ or $K = 29$, and also provide information about moves between nodes in each graph, which allows the use of coalescing in the allocation process. However, no spill cost information is provided, nor the code that represents the interference graph. This limits the tests in two ways. First when spill occurs, we can not know which variable will be spilled. To work around this problem we assumed that all nodes in the interference graph have $cost = 1$, therefore the node with higher degree is always chosen to spill. The second limitation is that we can not reconstruct the interference graph when spill occurs because there is no code information to make live analysis. In this way, the experiment only computes the effect of color flipping in the first round of the graph coloring algorithm if any spill occurs.

In order to test the efficiency of color flipping a Briggs' allocator without coalescing and where is possible enable color flipping was implemented without any framework dependence. The tests were performed assuming $K = 4, 8, 12, 16, 21/29$. The recursion level of the color flipping was set to 2, we try a recursion level > 2, but there was no significant improvement in the results - less than 0.5 %. The results are shown in Table 1. We observed that as the number of available register grows, the color flipping avoids more spills, this is due to the fact that more flipping opportunities become possible when there are more possibilities of coloring. However, even with $K = 4$ the reduction in

Table 1. Number of live range spills avoided for the Appel and George 27,921 interference graph samples.

K	Briggs - Total spills	Color flipping - Spills avoided	Reduction (%)
4	159,308	6,996	4.37
8	31,417	2,174	6.92
12	10,170	853	8.39
16	3,931	498	12.67
21/29	1,265	146	11.54

the number of live range spills is considerable. Another important observation is that our measurements in Table 1 are in terms of live range spills avoided, not in terms of load/store instructions reduction. As for each live range spilled some load/store instructions are inserted, if we were able to perform our measurements with Appel and George graph samples in terms of load/store reduction, an even better result would be obtained.

4.2 LLVM Experiments

To evaluate the quality of the code produced, the benchmark SPEC CPU2006 was compiled for architectures x86_64 and ARM-Cortex9. A comparison was made with the three main allocators of LLVM: basic, greedy and pbqp. It is difficult to talk about allocators basic and *greedy* because there is no official documentation about them. The best material found was an informal mail list between the author of both allocators and the LLVM community [22]. Based on this discussion and code itself, we can infer that both are hybrids allocators, using ordered intervals as the *extended linear scan* [24] but using allocation mechanisms similar of those used in the graph coloring. The basic uses a priority queue to separate unrestricted live ranges ($degree < k$) from restricted live ranges ($degree \geq k$) which is similar to the algorithm proposed by Chow and Hennessy [11,12]. The greedy is an extension of basic, which uses a form of iterative coalescing similar to George and Appel [15] with split on demand. This is the default allocator of LLVM. The pbqp allocator is based on quadratic problem solving implemented by Hames Scholz [18].

The results of SPEC CPU2006 benchmark compilation are shown in Tables 2 (x86_64) and 3 (ARM-Cortex9). Unlike the experiments performed in Sect. 4.1, in LLVM experiments the measurements are in terms of spill instructions (load/store). We notice that our allocator produced code with similar quality to LLVM allocators. In some cases much less spill code was inserted, e.g., 403.gcc, 400.perlbench. In 403.gcc for X86_64 (Table 2) was inserted 6,356 spills with *color flipping*, while all LLVM allocators inserted > 7300 spills. In 400.perlbench for ARM-CortexA9 (Table 3) was inserted 2,643 spills, while all LLVM allocators inserted > 3200 spills. We also notice that one of the best performances of *color flipping* was on the gcc benchmark. This may be due to the nature of the interfer-

ence graph of a compiler, since the samples of graphs of Appel and George, where
we achieve better results, also represented a compiler. Another important observation is that the *color flipping* was more effective in ARM-Cortex9 architecture,

Table 2. Amount of spill code inserted by each benchmark of SPEC CPU 2006 for
x86_64 architecture using Briggs', Color Flipping and LLVM's allocators.

Benchmark	Briggs	Color flipping	Reduction (%)	Greedy	Basic	PBQP
400.perlbench	2,957	2,943	0.47	3,789	3,568	3,192
401.bzip2	323	318	1.55	531	329	309
403.gcc	6,422	6,356	1.03	7,352	7,527	7,396
429.mcf	21	21	-	17	20	22
433.milc	663	663	-	612	693	677
444.namd	4,813	4,802	0.23	5,055	5,087	4,731
445.gobmk	2,230	2,227	0.13	2,365	2,325	2,230
450.soplex	1,255	1,255	-	1,127	1,310	1,261
456.hmmer	1,389	1,389	-	1,205	1,424	1,388
458.sjeng	196	196	-	236	217	196
464.h264	2,908	2,897	0.38	3,068	3,014	2,867
470.lbm	89	89	-	41	89	91
471.omnetpp	737	737	-	583	759	724
473.astar	190	190	-	176	197	189

Table 3. Amount of spill code inserted by each benchmark of SPEC CPU 2006 for
ARM-CortexA9 architecture using Briggs', Color Flipping and LLVM's allocators.

Benchmark	Briggs	Color flipping	Reduction (%)	Greedy	Basic	PBQP
400.perlbench	2,684	2,643	1.53	3,337	3,271	3,260
401.bzip2	571	556	2.63	739	573	539
403.gcc	6,661	6,536	1.88	7,589	7,605	7,694
429.mcf	30	30	-	31	36	31
433.milc	466	466	-	491	462	486
444.namd	3,655	3,652	0.08	4,926	3,759	3,569
445.gobmk	2,000	1,985	0.75	2,311	2,216	2,148
450.soplex	772	766	0.78	902	840	829
456.hmmer	723	721	0.28	855	755	783
458.sjeng	415	413	0.48	492	464	422
464.h264ref	3,799	3,779	0.53	3,984	3,981	3,818
470.lbm	28	28	-	22	32	28
471.omnetpp	192	191	0.51	239	196	236
473.astar	230	230	-	216	236	226

this suggests that *color flipping* may has a better performance in an environment with more *alias* [25]- while ARM has 289 register units, the X86_64 architecture has 241 register units. Finally we observe that *color flipping* always produced $\leq$ spills when compared to Briggs' allocator.

Based on the experiment of Sect. 4.1 we expected a greater spill reduction. There are two main causes for the results have been affected negatively. The first one is the register class issue. Most of modern architectures are irregular. This means that each live range can only be assigned to a specific set of registers. For example, a variable `int` can not be allocated to a class of registers of type `float`. The graph coloring algorithms are too abstract and do not deal with these issues in their original design. Modern research has sought to make this strategy generic enough to deal with these modern problems [25]. Unfortunately, the tests in Sect. 4.1 do not simulated this behavior. The second one is the spill cost issue. The tests with Appel and George graphs always spills the live range with greater degree, which differs from the spill heuristic used in real programs. This may causes unpredictable results.

5   Conclusion

In this work we presented a new spill code minimization technique called *color flipping*. Rather than try to partially spill a live range, the *color flipping* tries to recolor the interference graph, such that, a color is made available to the live range spilled. If *color flipping* succeeds no load/store instructions are inserted, that is, a machine register is assigned to the entire live range. Otherwise, the graph coloring algorithm proceeds normally with no change in the coloring of the interference graph. Another important advantage of using *color flipping* is that it can combined with other spill minimization techniques easily, which can improve the overall result of the final code.

Our experiments with the samples of Appel and George shown over 12 % of live range spills reduction, suggesting that *color flipping* is an effective technique to avoid spill code. However, in the experiments with the LLVM framework the performance of *color flipping* was not as effective: in most benchmarks there was a reduction $< 1\%$ of spill code.

In further tasks, we should investigate the causes of such performance. We notice that the second restriction occurred much more often in the LLVM experiment, then we will study ways to work around this restriction to achieve better results.

References

1. Appel, A.W.: Standard ml of New Jersey (1996). http://www.smlnj.org/. Accessed 18 Nov 2014
2. Appel, A.W., George, L.: Sample graph coloring problems (1996). https://www.cs.princeton.edu/appel/graphdata/. Accessed 18 Nov 2014

3. Barany, G., Krall, A.: Optimal and heuristic global code motion for minimal spilling. In: Jhala, R., De Bosschere, K. (eds.) Compiler Construction. LNCS, vol. 7791, pp. 21–40. Springer, Heidelberg (2013)

4. Bergner, P., Dahl, P., Engebretsen, D., O'Keefe, M.: Spill code minimization via interference region spilling. In: Proceedings of the ACM SIGPLAN 1997 Conference on Programming Language Design and Implementation, PLDI 1997, pp. 287–295. ACM, New York (1997). http://doi.acm.org/10.1145/258915.258941

5. Bernstein, D., Golumbic, M., Mansour, Y., Pinter, R., Goldin, D., Krawczyk, H., Nahshon, I.: Spill code minimization techniques for optimizing compliers. In: Proceedings of the ACM SIGPLAN 1989 Conference on Programming Language Design and Implementation. PLDI 1989, pp. 258–263. ACM, New York (1989). http://doi.acm.org/10.1145/73141.74841

6. Briggs, P., Cooper, K.D., Kennedy, K., Torczon, L.: Coloring heuristics for register allocation. In: Proceedings of the ACM SIGPLAN 1989 Conference on Programming language design and implementation. PLDI 1989, pp. 275–284. ACM, New York (1989). http://doi.acm.org/10.1145/73141.74843

7. Briggs, P.: Register allocation via graph coloring. Ph.D. thesis, Rice University (1992)

8. Briggs, P., Cooper, K.D., Torczon, L.: Rematerialization. In: Feldman, S.I., Wexelblat, R.L. (eds.) PLDI, pp. 311–321. ACM (1992)

9. Chaitin, G.J.: Register allocation & spilling via graph coloring. In: Proceedings of the 1982 SIGPLAN Symposium on Compiler Construction, SIGPLAN 1982, pp. 98–105. ACM, New York (1982). http://doi.acm.org/10.1145/800230.806984

10. Chaitin, G.J., Auslander, M.A., Chandra, A.K., Cocke, J., Hopkins, M.E., Markstein, P.W.: Register allocation via coloring. Comput. Lang. 6(1), 47–57 (1981)

11. Chow, F.C., Hennessy, J.L.: The priority-based coloring approach to register allocation. ACM Trans. Program. Lang. Syst. 12(4), 501–536 (1990). http://doi.acm.org/10.1145/88616.88621

12. Chow, F., Hennessy, J.: Register allocation by priority-based coloring. In: Proceedings of the 1984 SIGPLAN Symposium on Compiler Construction, SIGPLAN 1984, pp. 222–232. ACM, New York (1984). http://doi.acm.org/10.1145/502874.502896

13. Cooper, K.D., Simpson, L.T.: Live range splitting in a graph coloring register allocator. In: Koskimies, K. (ed.) CC 1998. LNCS, vol. 1383, pp. 174–187. Springer, Heidelberg (1998)

14. Gao, L., Shi, C.: An improved approach of register allocation via graph coloring. In: Proceedings of the SPIE, vol. 5683, no. 5, pp. 113–123, May 2005

15. George, L., Appel, A.W.: Iterated register coalescing. ACM Trans. Program. Lang. Syst. 18(3), 300–324 (1996). http://doi.acm.org/10.1145/229542.229546

16. Goodwin, D.W., Wilken, K.D.: Optimal and near-optimal global register allocations using 0–1 integer programming. Softw. Pract. Exper. 26(8), 929–965 (1996)

17. Govindarajan, R., Yang, H., Amaral, J.N., Zhang, C., Gao, G.R.: Minimum register instruction sequencing to reduce register spills in out-of-order issue superscalar architectures. IEEE Trans. Comput. 52(1), 4–20 (2003). http://dx.doi.org/10.1109/TC.2003.1159750

18. Hames, L., Scholz, B.: Nearly optimal register allocation with PBQP. In: Lightfoot, D.E., Ren, X.-M. (eds.) JMLC 2006. LNCS, vol. 4228, pp. 346–361. Springer, Heidelberg (2006)

19. Kempe, A.B.: On the geographical problem of the four colours. Am. J. Math. 2(3), 193–200 (1879)

20. Koseki, A., Komatsu, H., Nakatani, T.: Spill code minimization by spill code motion. In: Proceedings of the 22nd International Conference on Parallel Architectures and Compilation Techniques 0, p. 125 (2003)
21. Lattner, C., Adve, V.: Llvm: A compilation framework for lifelong program analysis & transformation. In: Proceedings of the International Symposium on Code Generation and Optimization: Feedback-directed and Runtime Optimization, CGO 2004, p. 75. IEEE Computer Society, Washington (2004). http://dl.acm.org/citation.cfm?id=977395.977673
22. Olesen, J.S.: Greedy register allocation in llvm 3.0 (2011). http://lists.cs.uiuc.edu/pipermail/llvmdev/2011-September/043511.html. Accessed 25 Aug 2014
23. Poletto, M., Sarkar, V.: Linear scan register allocation. ACM Trans. Program. Lang. Syst. **21**(5), 895–913 (1999). http://doi.acm.org/10.1145/330249.330250
24. Sarkar, V., Barik, R.: Extended linear scan: an alternate foundation for global register allocation. In: Adsul, B., Odersky, M. (eds.) CC 2007. LNCS, vol. 4420, pp. 141–155. Springer, Heidelberg (2007)
25. Smith, M.D., Ramsey, N., Holloway, G.: A generalized algorithm for graph-coloring register allocation. In: Proceedings of the ACM SIGPLAN 2004 Conference on Programming Language Design and Implementation, PLDI 2004, pp. 277–288. ACM, New York (2004). http://doi.acm.org/10.1145/996841.996875

Deadlocks as Runtime Exceptions

Rafael Lobo$^{(\boxtimes)}$ and Fernando Castor

Center of Informatics, Federal University of Pernambuco,
Recife, Brazil
{rbl,castor}@cin.ufpe.br
http://www.cin.ufpe.br/

Abstract. Deadlocks are a common type of concurrency bug. When a deadlock occurs, it is difficult to clearly determine whether there is an actual deadlock or if the application is slow or hanging due to a different reason. It is also difficult to establish the cause of the deadlock. In general, developers deal with deadlocks by using analysis tools, introducing application-specific deadlock detection mechanisms, or simply by using techniques to avoid the occurrence of deadlocks by construction. In this paper we propose a different approach. We believe that if deadlocks manifest at runtime, as exceptions, programmers will be able to identify these deadlocks in an accurate and timely manner. We leverage two insights to make this practical: (i) most deadlocks occurring in real systems involve only two threads acquiring two locks (TTTL deadlocks); and (ii) it's possible to detect TTTL deadlocks efficiently enough for most practical systems. We conducted a study on bug reports and found that more than 90 % of identified deadlocks were indeed TTTL. We extended Java's `ReentrantLock` class to detect TTTL deadlocks and measured the performance overhead of this approach with a conservative benchmark. For applications whose execution time is not dominated by locking, the overhead is estimated as below 6 %. Empirical usability evaluation in two experiments showed that students finished tasks 16.87 % to 30.7 % faster on the average using our approach with the lock being the most significant factor behind it, and, in one of the experiments answers were significantly more accurate (81.25 % more correct bugs found).

Keywords: Deadlock · Concurrency · Exception handling · Empirical studies

1 Introduction

Real-world applications use concurrency to do computation in parallel with multiple threads/processes taking more advantage of multicore processors. Unfortunately, concurrent code is difficult to write correctly, as it is well documented [1]. Deadlocks are a very common type of error in concurrent systems [1]. Deadlocks manifest when threads are waiting each other in a cycle, where each thread is waiting for another thread to release its desired lock. This produces a never-ending wait. Although there are two well-documented types of deadlocks,

© Springer International Publishing Switzerland 2015
A. Pardo and S.D. Swierstra (Eds.): SBLP 2015, LNCS 9325, pp. 96–111, 2015.
DOI: 10.1007/978-3-319-24012-1_8

resource deadlocks and communication deadlocks [2,3], in this work our focus is on resource deadlocks, e.g., deadlocks that stem from threads attempting to obtain exclusive access to resources, and whenever the term *deadlock* is used we implicitly mean resource deadlock.

In practice, developers employ a number of approaches to deal with deadlocks: (i) static program analyses [4,7–9]; (ii) dynamic program analyses [10–14,16]; (iii) application-specific deadlock detection infrastructures [19]; (iv) techniques to guarantee the absence of deadlocks by construction [4]; (v) model checking [17]. The first two approaches are known to be heavyweight. In addition, the former often produces many false positives. The third approach has limited applicability and often imposes a high runtime overhead. The fourth approach has a low cost but cannot be employed in cases where it is not feasible to order lock acquisitions nor use non-blocking locking primitives. Finally, model checking is a powerful solution but has limited scalability when applied in the context of real programs. It also has limited generality, since some programs with side effects simply cannot be model checked.

In this paper we advocate an approach that complements the aforementioned ones. In summary, we believe deadlocks should not fail silently but instead their occurrence should be signaled as exceptions at runtime. To make this vision possible, we leverage two insights: (i) the vast majority of existing deadlocks occur between two threads attempting to acquire two locks (as reported by other authors [1] and confirmed by us in Sect. 2); and (ii) it is possible to efficiently introduce deadlock detection for these two-thread, two-lock deadlocks (TTTL deadlocks) within the locking mechanism itself, incurring in an overhead that is low for applications whose execution time is not dominated by locking. We present a new type of lock that automatically checks for TTTL deadlocks at runtime and, if one is found, throws an exception indicating the problem. We have implemented this approach as an extension to Java's `ReentrantLock` class. Deadlock exceptions are already supported in programming languages such as Haskell [5] and Go [6] but they focus on different types of deadlocks. Similarly, runtime exceptions for data races have been proposed [15].

We present data from an empirical study showing that our assumption about the prevalence of TTTL deadlocks holds in practice. This confirms the findings of a previous study that focused on concurrency bugs in general [1]. To evaluate our approach, we conducted two controlled experiments. In both cases, subjects using these new locks were able to detect deadlocks significantly faster than subjects not using them. Furthermore, in one of the studies, this approach helped the subjects to more accurately identify the causes of the deadlock. We also show that our approach has an overhead that, while non-negligible, is low for applications whose execution time is not dominated by locking.

2   Bug Reports Study

Attempting to generalize deadlock detection at runtime does not seem feasible from a performance viewpoint, since existing dynamic analyses take considerable time [11]. But previous bug reports study [1] found that 30 out of 31 deadlock bug reports involved at most two resources. We suspected TTTL deadlocks were more common in real world systems than more complex deadlocks, so we investigated this further. This section presents the results of this investigation.

2.1   Data Collection

We selected three open source projects to investigate: Lucene, Eclipse and Open-JDK. Lucene[1] is a text search engine library. Eclipse[2] is one of the most popular IDEs for java developers. OpenJDK[3] is an open-source implementation of the Java Platform. These three projects share some key similarities: they're mostly written in Java; they have immense bug report repositories with easy tools to search into them; and lastly, their bug reports were usually well discussed and contained enough context that allowed us to classify them with some confidence, which was very important in this study.

In total, we collected 541 bug reports containing the word *deadlock* on their titles or on their descriptions. In Lucene, we found 27 closed issues of type "bug" in module "lucene-core".[4] In Eclipse, we found 406 resolved issues with resolution "fixed".[5] In OpenJDK, we found 108 issues of type "bug" on module "JDK" with resolution "fixed" and status "resolved".[6] We then proceeded to calculate the sample size that would allow us to have 95 % of confidence level and 5 % sampling error, which resulted in 225 bugs. Thus we created a random sample of that size to analyze further [7].

2.2   Data Labeling

We defined a set of fields to classify for each bug analyzed in the sample. First, we define a category. Then complete other fields based on how much we could understand of each bug report, like the number of threads involved, number of resources involved, type of locking mechanism used, and so on.

We have four different values for the category field. Category A indicates that we are confident this is a resource deadlock. Thus, we should be able to describe the number of threads and locks that were involved. In contrast, category B represents the opposite: it is certainly not a resource deadlock. The reported bug is a communication deadlock, due to evidence of lost notify/signal in the bug context or anything else that supports it was not a resource deadlock. Category C refers to all the false-positive results: the term *deadlock* was used as a synonym of "hanging" or an "infinite loop", or to just mention another deadlock bug as a

---

[1] Lucene: http://lucene.apache.org/.
[2] Eclipse: https://eclipse.org/.
[3] OpenJDK: http://openjdk.java.net/.
[4] Lucene bug reports list: http://goo.gl/DhVI3t.
[5] Eclipse bug reports: http://goo.gl/qQnrEm.
[6] OpenJDK bug reports: http://goo.gl/xYFfsO.
[7] Bug reports sample: http://goo.gl/zNsIGz.

reference, not as a cause of the current bug. Lastly, category D is set for all bugs that we could not understand clearly, due to a lack of evidence or discussion.

2.3 Results Analysis

Initially we consider only bugs we clearly identified, that is, bugs that were not labeled as category D. In Table 1 (second column), we can see in that from all resource deadlocks, 92.07 % of them are indeed TTTL deadlocks. Another interesting finding is that 75.93 % of all deadlocks are indeed resource deadlocks.

Table 1. Labeled categories and estimations

Category	Number of bugs	Estimated
A	101	146
A and TTTL	93	134
B	32	46
C	23	33
D	69	0

If we now consider bugs we could not clearly classify, we can make some estimations of how many of them would be resource deadlocks and TTTL deadlocks. The first estimate is the worse case scenario, that is, all bugs in category D should be in category A but none of them would be TTTL deadlocks. In this case, only 54.7 % of resource deadlocks would be TTTL deadlocks. If we look at the best case scenario, that is, all bugs in D would be TTTL deadlocks, then it would be 95.29 % instead. However none of these two scenarios seems realistic. We believe that a more realistic scenario would be to assume that bugs in category D are distributed roughly in the same way as those in categories A, B, and C. If that is the case (last column of Table 1), out of all resource deadlocks, we estimate that 91.7 % of them would also be TTTL deadlocks. Thus TTTL deadlocks are certainly the most popular type of resource deadlocks, amounting to more than 9 out of every 10 resource deadlocks. This result makes it evident that an approach to automatically detect these deadlocks has practical value.

2.4 Threats to Validity

Only one of the authors labeled all bug reports due to constraints on time and lack of resources. In counterpart, having only one reviewer makes it easier to guarantee that all bug reports were reviewed following the exact same procedure, but we would have preferred to have at least one more reviewer to label each bug independently and use it as a way to double check the labels accuracy. Furthermore, one factor that might limit generalization of these findings is that all projects we looked were written in Java and different programming languages may have different distribution of deadlock bugs.

3 Deadlock Detection

In this section we present the proposed approach. We extend the notion of lock by making locks responsible for both detecting TTTL deadlocks and raising exceptions whenever such deadlocks occur. In this section we present an algorithm implementing this extended notion of lock and show that our algorithm guarantees that (i) every TTTL deadlock is detected; and (ii) if an exception reporting a deadlock is raised, it must stem from the occurrence of a TTTL deadlock.

We have modified the default implementation of Java's *ReentrantLock* to allow efficient runtime detection of TTTL deadlocks. It works as follows:

1. Each lock has a pointer to a thread, the owner of the lock, or `null` when no thread owns that lock.
2. Each lock has an integer to represent its current state: 0 means the lock is free and no thread owns it (the *unlocked* state), 1 means there is a thread that owns the lock (the *locked* state). For simplicity, we are only interested on these two states. Nonetheless, in the implementation of *ReentrantLock*, each time a thread owner acquires the same lock, this state would be incremented, and decremented each time the thread releases it.
3. Each thread has a thread-local list of pointers to locks it currently owns.
4. Each lock has a waiting queue of threads that are waiting to acquire it. Whenever a thread tries to obtain a lock when it's already acquired, the thread will add itself to the waiting queue before parking. Upon the event of releasing the lock, the owner of that lock will look for the first thread in the waiting queue and unpark it.
5. When a thread wants to acquire a lock, it will swap the current state to *locked* if the current state is *unlocked* atomically.
   (a) If the thread fails, it must be because the lock is already owned by some other thread, then it will add itself on the waiting queue for that lock. Finally, the thread will park.
   (b) Otherwise, the thread will set itself as the current owner of that lock and also add this lock to its thread-local list of pointers of locks it owns.
6. When a thread is about to release a lock, the current owner pointer of that lock is set to `null` and that lock is also removed from the thread-local list of owned locks. Finally, the lock state is changed to *unlocked*.
7. Before parking, a thread will check whether there is a deadlock. When the current thread is unable to acquire its desired lock, it must be because another thread already owns it. It is possible to know who is the owner of any lock, so the current thread identifies the owner of its desired lock as the conflicting thread. Then the current thread will search on each lock of its list of owned locks if the conflicting thread is waiting for it.
   (a) If positive, then we have a circular dependency (current thread is stuck waiting for its desired lock and the conflicting thread is stuck waiting for a lock the current thread owns) and thus a deadlock exception will be raised.
   (b) Otherwise, the thread parks.

We take advantage of the current algorithm employed by *ReentrantLock* and some of its guarantees listed below to avoid the need to introduce extra synchronization mechanisms or costly atomic operations during deadlock detection:

1. The operation of swapping the state of a lock from *unlocked* to *locked* must be done atomically by the thread, so only one thread can be successful at a time.
2. A thread will only park when it is guaranteed that some other thread can unpark it. Missing notifications will never happen and concurrent uses of park and unpark on the same thread will be resolved gracefully.
3. Inserts on each lock's waiting queue must be done atomically. If multiple threads concurrently attempt to insert themselves in the waiting queue on the same lock, they will both succeed eventually but the exact order of insertions is not important.
4. Once the last element in the waiting queue of a lock is read, it should be safe to read all threads in the waiting queue that arrived before the last element. Since the thread who reads the waiting queues is also the one who blocks every thread waiting on the queues, we can guarantee the only updates that could happen concurrently are new insertions at the end of each queue. However insertions in the end of the queue are not important once a last element pointer is obtained.

Lemma 1. *The proposed protocol can always detect TTTL deadlocks.*

Proof. By way of contradiction, suppose not and a TTTL deadlock occurred without it being detected. Lets assume that threads A and B have both acquired locks a and b respectively, as follows:

$$write_A(state_a = locked) \rightarrow write_A(owner_a = A) \tag{1}$$

$$write_B(state_b = locked) \rightarrow write_B(owner_b = B) \tag{2}$$

In the above expressions, '$x \rightarrow y$' indicates that event x happened before event y. Notation '$write_B(owner_b = B)$' indicates that thread B wrote to variable $owner_b$ the value B. And now each thread will attempt to acquire the opposing lock: thread A is trying to acquire lock b and thread B is trying to acquire lock a, as follows:

$$read_A(state_b == locked) \rightarrow write_A(waiting\_queue_b.insert(A)) \tag{3}$$

$$read_B(state_a == locked) \rightarrow write_B(waiting\_queue_a.insert(B)) \tag{4}$$

The notation '$read_A(state_b == locked)$' indicates that thread A read variable $state_b$ and obtained value *locked*. If a TTTL deadlock happened, then both threads are now parked and all previous equations should be correct. But before parking, each thread must check for deadlock by inspecting each lock it owns if the opposing thread is on its waiting queue. As we initially assumed no deadlock exception has been raised, then both threads are parked and also the following equations must be correct:

$$read_A(owner_b == B) \rightarrow read_A(waiting\_queue_a.contains(B) == false) \quad (5)$$

$$read_B(owner_a == A) \rightarrow read_B(waiting\_queue_b.contains(A) == false) \quad (6)$$

The problem with the previous equations is that they both cannot be true simultaneously. Before checking for deadlock, each thread must add itself on the waiting queue of its desired lock. If it holds that the opposing thread is not in the waiting queue yet, then it must be because it did not start to check for deadlock yet, thus a contradiction.   □

Lemma 2. *The proposed protocol never raises a deadlock exception for a non-existent TTTL deadlock.*

Proof. By way of contradiction, assume the opposite: a deadlock exception was raised and there is no real TTTL deadlock. Exactly one of the following equations must be true in order to raise a deadlock exception (if both were true at the same time, an actual deadlock would have occurred):

$$read_A(owner_b == B) \rightarrow read_A(waiting\_queue_a.contains(B) == true) \quad (7)$$

$$read_B(owner_a == A) \rightarrow read_B(waiting\_queue_b.contains(A) == true) \quad (8)$$

Suppose without loss of generality that the first equation is true. It means that thread B is waiting for lock a and it is also the owner of lock b. If it is on the waiting queue, that thread is either parked already or about to park and in both cases thread B is going to depend on the release of lock a to proceed. However, as we have seem previously, thread A at this point is also about to park and is checking for a deadlock. If this condition holds, we have a circular dependency between threads A and B, a real TTTL deadlock, thus we have a contradiction.   □

3.1   Extension: Raising Exceptions in All Threads

The protocol we presented guarantees that an exception is raised in at least one of the threads involved in a deadlock. A safer approach, however, would be to have exceptions raised in both threads involved in the deadlock. In this section we describe an extension to the protocol that provides this guarantee. This does not affect how deadlock is detected but what should be done after a deadlock is detected. Thus, does not impact the correctness of the protocol. The proposed extension comprises the following:

1. Each lock has a list of tainted threads. This list should only be read or updated by the owner of that lock, allowing immunity from interference without any extra synchronization cost.
2. Once a deadlock is detected and the current thread is about to raise a deadlock exception, it already knows which thread is conflicting with itself and which lock that thread desires. The current thread (the owner of the desired lock) will add this conflicting thread to the tainted threads list for that lock. After that, the deadlock exception is raised.

3. When the conflicting thread is unparked and finally acquires its desired lock (it becomes the owner of that lock), then it is allowed to read the list of tainted threads. If this thread identifies itself in this list, then it must be because it was part of a deadlock before, so it removes its reference from the list and also raises a deadlock exception.
4. Every operation on the list of tainted threads of any lock (either reading or inserting values) should be followed up by some cleanup on all references to threads that are no longer running.

That is sufficient to force both threads to raise exceptions when only one of them would raise an exception in the initial protocol. The latter only raises exception on both threads if they simultaneously reach the point where they check for deadlocks. However, for this particular case, this change introduces a different problem: dangling references. If each thread adds their conflicting thread to the lists of tainted threads of the locks they own, but none of them is able to acquire their respective desired locks (as in *item 3*), both threads will leave their references behind for others to cleanup (as in *item 4*). We minimize this issue by cleaning these references as soon as any thread acquires the lock.

3.2   Implementation

The modified OpenJDK *ReentrantLock* version to implement this algorithm is available in our code repository [18]. Further implementation details were omitted here for brevity.

4   Evaluation

In this section we present an evaluation of our approach. Our evaluation comprises two parts: (i) a usability evaluation involving two experiments with two groups of students (Sect. 4.1); and (ii) a preliminary analysis of the performance overhead of our approach (Sect. 4.2). The exact input, instructions, and any additional document we have used in this section are available at [18].

4.1   Usability Evaluation

We ran empirical evaluation to measure the efficiency of deadlock exceptions with regard to problem solving speed and accuracy. We defined two research questions for this evaluation: **RQ1.** Is the time spent to identify the bug reduced using our implementation? **RQ2.** Is the accuracy in the identification of the causes of a deadlock bug improved for developers using our approach? For the second question, each answer was evaluated based on three criteria with three possible values each: 0 for absence, 0.5 for partially present and 1 for fully present. First criteria, A, stands for "correctly classified problem as deadlock"; second criteria, B, means "classified problem as different from deadlock"; and lastly, C means "correctly identified method calls involved in the deadlock". Whenever

$(A - B) + C \geq 1.5$ is true, we defined it as a correct answer (that is, whenever the bug was described as deadlock and at least one of the methods involved in the deadlock were identified correctly).

We wrote two programs with different levels of complexity which were presented in the same order for all subjects. The first program, known as *Bank*, contained 4 classes spread among 4 files, 3 threads, 3 explicit locks, and a mean of 82 lines of code per file. The second program, known as *Eclipse*, had 15 classes spread in 11 files, 4 threads, 5 explicit locks, and a mean of 40 lines of code per file. Each program could use either *LockA* or *LockB*, where *LockA* was our implementation with deadlock detection on at least one thread involved in a deadlock, while *LockB* was just the default *ReentrantLock* implementation. Each student was assigned to either group A or B randomly. In group A, students would start with *LockA* in the first program but use *LockB* on the second program; meanwhile, in group B students would have the locks in opposite order.

The two experiments had similar setups but differed in terms of the subjects. For the first experiment, the subjects comprised a group of third-year undergraduate students who underwent an 18-hour concurrent programming course. The course included a number of programming assignments. The experiment was conducted as a test for the course. The subjects of the second experiment were graduate students enrolled in master's degree or PhD program attending a 40-hour Parallel Programming course with a focus on algorithms and data structures. They had classes about advanced concepts of parallel programming and had practical exercises, including implementing a number of different locking approaches. The participants in the second experiment were all volunteers and were not required to take part in it. Also, for both experiments, the assignments were the same. It asked students to identify any problems they could with the provided programs. All students started the experiment with program *Bank*. When they finished, they received the second program, *Eclipse*. When a student finished one of the programs, we set a timestamp on it. The timestamp was written based on a chronometer visible to everyone in the laboratory. For the first group (undergraduate students), we allowed 90 min per program. For the second group (graduate students), we allowed 60 min per program.

Time Analysis. We defined the following hypothesis to answer **RQ1**:

$$H_0 : \mu_{TimeLockA} \geq \mu_{TimeLockB} \tag{9}$$

$$H_1 : \mu_{TimeLockA} < \mu_{TimeLockB} \tag{10}$$

We used Latin Square Design [24] to control two factors that might affect the metrics: subjects and program complexity. Programs *Bank* and *Eclipse* had complexity easy and difficult respectively, while *LockA* and *LockB* were the two possible treatments we wanted to compare. Since we had N subjects, 2 programs and 2 possible treatments, we disposed subjects in rows and programs in columns of latin squares, randomly assigning in each cell of the square a treatment that could be *LockA* or *LockB*, but also guaranteeing that for any given row or column in this square, each treatment appeared only once. Consequently, we have replication, local control and randomization which are the three principles of experiment design [24]. Time analysis was conducted with R Statistical Software using the inputs extracted from each day. We used the linear model described in Fig. 1 that considers the effect of different factors on the response variable as proposed by other authors [21], including the effect between each replica and treatment [20].

$$Y_{lijk} = \mu + \tau_l + \tau\alpha_{li} + \beta_j + \gamma_k + \tau\gamma_{lk} + \epsilon_{lijk}$$

Y_{lijk} - response of l_{th} replica, i_{th} student, j_{th} program, k_{th} lock
τ_l - effect of l_{th} replica
$\tau\alpha_{li}$ - effect of interaction between l_{th} replica and i_{th} student
β_j - effect of j_{th} program
γ_k - effect of k_{th} lock
$\tau\gamma_{lk}$ - effect of interaction between l_{th} replica and k_{th} lock
ϵ_{lijk} - random error

Fig. 1. Regression model.

Initially, we plotted box-plot graphics shown in Fig. 2 for both experiments and calculated the means for time spent in Tables 2 and 3, where we can observe that students finished the exercise faster on the average when using our approach: 16.87 % less time on the first group and 30.70 % less on the second group. Then we ran Box-Cox transformation to reduce anomalies such as non-additivity and non-normality. The value of λ at the maximum point in the curve drawn by box-cox function in R was not approximately 1 ($\lambda = 5$), thus we should apply the transformation: on our regression model, Y_{lijk} should be powered to λ. We did the same on the second experiment as $\lambda = 1.3636$.

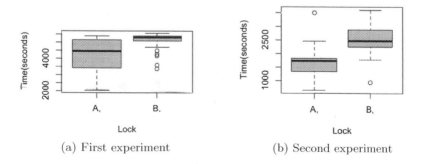

(a) First experiment   (b) Second experiment

Fig. 2. Box-plot on both experiment days

Table 2. First group's time spent

	Time spent (mean)
LockA	4227.800 s
LockB	5086.367 s

Table 3. Second group's time spent

	Time spent (mean)
LockA	1737.714 s
LockB	2507.714 s

Table 4. First experiment ANOVA results.

	Df	Sum Sq	Mean Sq	F value	p-value
Replica	14	3.8633e + 37	2.7595e + 36	1.6553	0.1784197
Program	1	4.1460e + 36	4.1460e + 36	2.4869	0.1371197
Lock	1	3.9489e + 37	3.9489e + 37	23.6873	0.0002492 ***
Replica: Student	15	4.1013e + 37	2.7342e + 36	1.6401	0.1808595
Replica: Lock	14	2.4033e + 37	1.7166e + 36	1.0297	0.4785520
Residuals	14	2.3340e + 37	1.6671e + 36		

After applying Box-Cox transformation, we ran Tukey Test of Additivity that checks whether effect model is additive. If the model was additive, then rows and columns of each latin square wouldn't affect significantly the response [24]. Now consider the hypothesis where the null hypothesis (H_0) says the model is additive and alternative hypothesis (H_1) says the opposite. In the first experiment, model was additive as we obtained p-value of 0.514 which is not lower than 0.05 and we couldn't reject H_0; similarly for the second experiment, the model was also additive as p-value found was 0.914.

Finally, we ran the ANOVA (ANalysis Of VAriance) test which compares the effect of treatments on the response variable, providing an approximated p-value for every associated factor. When a variable has p-$value < 0.05$, it means that factor was significant to the response. Tables 4 and 5 shows **the most important factor as the type of *Lock* for both experiments**, allowing us to reject our null hypothesis defined for **RQ1**. Thus, considering this result and the box plots in Fig. 2, we can say that the use of our locks promoted faster identification of deadlocks.

Accuracy Analysis. We used the number of correct answers using each lock to measure accuracy, so we defined the following hypothesis to answer **RQ2**.

$$H_0 : \mu_{CorrectAnswersLockA} \leq \mu_{CorrectAnswersLockB} \tag{11}$$

$$H_1 : \mu_{CorrectAnswersLockA} > \mu_{CorrectAnswersLockB} \tag{12}$$

To compare the accuracy of the subjects using Java's regular `ReentrantLock` and our modified implementation, we employed Fisher's exact test [25]. We could not use ANOVA because the data for accuracy is categorical (Correct vs. Incorrect) instead of numerical. Applying Fisher's exact test on data from Tables 6

Table 5. Second experiment ANOVA results.

	Df	Sum Sq	Mean Sq	F value	Pr(>F)
Replica	6	2576883250	429480542	14.1891	0.0025793 **
Program	1	6875586	6875586	0.2272	0.6505035
Lock	1	1958179433	1958179433	64.6938	0.0001975 ***
Replica: student	7	2328154077	332593440	10.9881	0.0047601 **
Replica: lock	6	823830276	137305046	4.5362	0.0441188 *
Residuals	6	181610625	30268438		

Table 6. First group's accuracy

	Correct	Incorrect
LockA	29	2
LockB	16	15

Table 7. Second group's accuracy

	Correct	Incorrect
LockA	13	1
LockB	10	4

and 7, we can see that undergraduate students results presented a two-tailed P value equals 0.0004: the association between rows (groups) and columns (outcomes) was considered to be extremely statistically significant; consequently, it suggests that an improvement on accuracy occurred due to the use of the proposed approach, where it had 81.25 % more correct answers. However graduate students results only had 30 % more correct answers with a two-tailed P value equals 0.3259, which does not represent statistically significant evidence.

Although we cannot draw strong conclusions regarding improved accuracy, we found some interesting behavior. Some students in the second group were greatly experienced on concurrent programming and they knew how to efficiently find a deadlock using the tools available in their IDE of choice, thus being able to finish the tasks really quickly for both problems. This observation allows us to hypothetize that deadlock exceptions are more helpful for less experienced programmers, but we leave investigation of this matter for future work.

Threats to Validity. We must consider a few remarks regarding the validity of our results. First remark: we could have used automated process to handle timestamps rather than manually writing their name with it on the whiteboard once they finished a question to keep track of time limit per subject later; this could potentially reduce overhead and increase timestamp precision. Secondly, the first group did this experiment in replacement of their actual exam might have impacted the time we measured. We noticed some students spent more time on each question by purpose. We believe that they were reluctant to ask for the next question because they still had plenty of time left and they wanted to make sure it was correct. We did not notice such behavior with the second group of students and we believe it is because they did not have the same pressure to deliver correct results as the first group had. Third remark is related to programs' complexity: the ones we used to evaluate the students are considerably easier to

understand than most programs in real world, but unfortunately we could not use
any real world scenario as students would not be able to finish each assignment
in time; with that in mind, we created two questions based on real world bugs
we found on our bug report studies.

Last remark is about whether we are able to draw conclusions based on
students data: some studies suggest that using students as subjects is as good
as using industry professionals [23]; Runes ran an experiment which shows that
there's not much significant differences between undergraduate, graduate and
industry professionals, with the exception that undergraduate students often
take more time to complete the tasks [22].

4.2 Performance Overhead

We conducted a preliminary set of experiments to analyze the overhead of
our approach. We compared our deadlock-safe implementation with the original `ReentrantLock` implementation available in the JDK and with Eclipse's
deadlock-safe `OrderedLock` [19]. `OrderedLock` is similar our approach in the
sense that it attempts to detect deadlocks at runtime. However, it aims to be
general, detecting N-thread deadlocks without much concern for performance.
OrderedLock deeply relies on Eclipse's code architecture. So, in order to use it
in our evaluation, we had to perform some small code changes, removing only
Eclipse-specific bits that did not affect the core functionality of `OrderedLock`.
The source code for these lock implementations is available elsewhere [18].

We developed a synthetic benchmark that creates N threads that perform
additions to ten integer counters where each increment in a counter is protected
by explicit locks. Each thread would have to increment its corresponding counter
1000 times before finishing its execution and the counters were evenly distributed
across the threads. Therefore, each counter will have exactly $(N/10)$ threads
doing increments on it and higher values of N result in higher contention, that
is, more threads will compete against each other for a particular counter. In this
preliminary evaluation, we have conducted measurements for values of N equal
to 10, 50, 100, and 200. Since each thread in the benchmark never acquires more
than one lock at the same time, deadlocks cannot occur. We emphasize that
this setup is very conservative, since every operation that each thread performs
requires locking. Thus, the obtained overhead will be a worst-case estimate and
thus much higher than one would encounter in a real-world application [26].
The measurements were made on an Intel CoreTM i7 3632QM Processor (6Mb
Cache, 2.2GHz) running Ubuntu 12.04.4 LTS and each cell in Table 8 is the
average of 50 executions (preceded by 20 executions that served as a warm-up).

The difference of results between our implementation and the original ReentrantLock gives a range of increased time from about 50 % to 90 %. Meanwhile,
OrderedLock performed a lot worse, reaching a 8446.3 % increase in time for the
worst case. To get a rough estimate of the impact that this overhead would have
on actual application execution time, we analyzed the results obtained by Lozi et
al. [26]. The authors profiled 19 real-world applications and small benchmarks in

Table 8. Benchmark time measurements (in seconds)

# Threads	ReentrantLock	ReentrantLock modified	OrderedLock
10	0.084184	0.105729	0.159503
50	0.089094	0.136507	1.094718
100	0.090978	0.159541	3.395974
200	0.131739	0.194075	11.258714

order to measure the time these systems spend on their critical sections. Worst-case results ranged between 0.3 % and 92.7 %. If we consider the average time spent on the critical sections of 12 of these systems, the impact of our approach on the overall execution time would be **less than 6 % in the worst case**. The remaining cases are extreme, in the sense that these systems spend more time in their critical sections than out of them [26].

5   Conclusion

In this work, we investigated deadlock bug reports in open source projects and confirmed a previous study claim that TTTL deadlocks are the most frequent case of deadlock (92.07 % of all resource deadlocks we identified). We modified Java's *ReentrantLock* and provided a lightweight version of it that detects TTTL deadlock in runtime. We measured its performance overhead with a very conservative benchmark and we estimate our cost to be less than 6 % for worse case on real world applications. Finally, we did an empirical evaluation to measure its usability and we found that deadlock exceptions speeds up finding deadlock bugs in code, and we also found some non-conclusive evidence showing that it may also improve accuracy of deadlock bug reports, but we leave for future work to verify whether this last observation is actually true.

Acknowledgments. We thank feedback from anonymous reviewers and from SPG group at CIn/UFPE. Rafael was supported by a grant provided by CAPES. Fernando is supported by CNPq/Brazil (304755/2014-1, 487549/2012-0 and 477139/2013-2), FACEPE/Brazil (APQ- 0839-1.03/14) and INES (CNPq 573964/2008-4, FACEPE APQ-1037-1.03/08, and FACEPE APQ-0388-1.03/14).

References

1. Lu, S., et al.: Learning from mistakes: a comprehensive study on real world concurrency bug characteristics. In: ACM Sigplan Notices, vol. 43, no. 3. ACM (2008)
2. Singhal, M.: Deadlock detection in distributed systems. Computer **22**(11), 37–48 (1989)
3. Knapp, E.: Deadlock detection in distributed databases. ACM Computing Surveys (CSUR) **19**(4), 303–328 (1987)

4. Marino, D., et al.: Detecting deadlock in programs with data-centric synchronization. In: 2013 35th International Conference on Software Engineering (ICSE). IEEE (2013)
5. Marlow, S.: Parallel and Concurrent Programming in Haskell: Techniques for Multicore and Multithreaded Programming. O'Reilly, Aug 2013
6. Aimonetti, M.: Go Bootcamp: Chap. 8 - Concurrency. http://www.golang bootcamp.com/book/concurrency
7. Engler, D., Ashcraft, K.: RacerX: effective, static detection of race conditions and deadlocks. SIGOPS Oper. Syst. Rev. 37(5), 237–252 (2003)
8. Shanbhag, V.K.: Deadlock-detection in java-library using static-analysis. In: Asia-PacificSoftware Engineering Conference, pp. 361–368 (2008)
9. Williams, A., Thies, W., Awasthi, P.: Static deadlock detection for java libraries. In: Gao, X.-X. (ed.) ECOOP 2005. LNCS, vol. 3586, pp. 602–629. Springer, Heidelberg (2005)
10. Da Luo, Z., Das, R., Qi, Y.: Multicore sdk: a practical and efficient deadlock detector for real-world applications. In: 2011 IEEE Fourth International Conference on Software Testing, Verification and Validation (ICST). IEEE (2011)
11. Cai, Y., Chan, W.K.: MagicFuzzer: scalable deadlock detection for large-scale applications. In: Proceedings of the 2012 International Conference on Software Engineering. IEEE Press (2012)
12. Pyla, H.K., Varadarajan, S.: Avoiding deadlock avoidance. In: Proceedings of the 19th International Conference on Parallel Architectures and Compilation Techniques. ACM (2010)
13. Pyla, H.K., Varadarajan, S.: Transparent runtime deadlock elimination. In: Proceedings of the 21st International Conference on Parallel Architectures and Compilation Techniques, PACT 2012, pp. 477–478. ACM, New York (2012)
14. Pyla, H.K.: Safe Concurrent Programming and Execution (2013)
15. Biswas, S., et al.: Efficient, Software-Only Data Race Exceptions (2015)
16. Qin, F., Tucek, J., Zhou, Y., Sundaresan, J.: Rx: Treating bugs as allergies–a safe method to survive software failures. ACM Trans. Comput. Syst., 25(3), August 2007
17. Havelund, K., Pressburger, T.: Model checking java programs using java pathfinder. Int. J. Softw. Tools Technol. Transf. 2(4), 366–381 (2000)
18. Java's ReentrantLock with DeadlockException. https://github.com/rafael brandao/java-lock-deadlock-exception
19. Eclipe's OrderedLock class description. Documentation http://cct.lsu.edu/ rguidry/ecl31docs/api/org/eclipse/core/internal/jobs/OrderedLock.html
20. Sanchez, I.: Latin Squares and its applications on software engineering. Master's thesis, Federal University of Pernambuco, Recife, Brazil (2011)
21. Accioly, P.: Comparing different testing strategies for software product lines. Master's thesis, Federal University of Pernambuco, Recife, Brazil (2012)
22. Runeson, P.: Using students as experiement subjects - an analysis on graduate and freshmen student data. In: Proceedings of the 7th International Conference on Empirical Assessment in Software Engineering. Keele University, UK, pp. 95–102 (2003)
23. Staron, M.: Using students as subjects in experiments - a quantitative analysis of the influence of experimentation on students' learning process. In: CSEE & T, pp. 221–228. IEEE Computer Society (2007)
24. Box, G.E.P., Hunter, J.S., Hunter, W.G.: Statistics for Experimenters: Design, Innovation, and Discovery. Wiley-Interscience (2005)

25. Agresti, A.: A survey of exact inference for contingency tables. Statistical Science, pp. 131–153 (1992)
26. Lozi, J.-P., David, F., Thomas, G., Lawall, J., Muller, G.: Remote core locking: migrating critical-section execution to improve the performance of multithreaded applications. In: Proceedings of the 2012 USENIX Annual Technical Conference (USENIX ATC 2012), Berkeley, CA, USA (2012)

Model-Driven Engineering Based on Attribute Grammars

Daniel Calegari$^{(\boxtimes)}$ and Marcos Viera

Universidad de la República, Montevideo, Uruguay
{dcalegar,mviera}@fing.edu.uy

Abstract. The Model-Driven Engineering (MDE) paradigm proposes the construction of software based on an abstraction from its complexity by defining models, and on a (semi)automatic construction process driven by model transformations. In this paper we propose the use of attribute grammars for the specification of QVT-like (Query/View/Transformation) relational model transformations. We also present how the syntax and semantics of models can be represented, and we discuss the practical implications of this approach through the development of a case study.

Keywords: Model-Driven Engineering · Attribute grammars · QVT · Haskell

1 Introduction

The use of a model-centric approach for the specification of a system, and of automated mechanisms for its construction, improves efficiency on the whole process. The Model-Driven Engineering (MDE, [1]) paradigm is based on these practices. It envisions a software development life-cycle driven by models representing different views of the system to be constructed and model transformations providing a (semi)automatic construction process. Models are defined from metamodels, i.e. a model which introduces the syntax and semantics of certain domain-specific kind of models. The relation between a model and its metamodel is called conformance. A model transformation is basically the automatic generation of a target model from a source model, according to a set of rules that describe how certain elements in the source model can be transformed into certain others in the target model. The Object Management Group (OMG) has conducted a standardization process of languages and defined the MetaObject Facility (MOF, [2]) for metamodeling, and the Query/View/Transformation Relations (QVT-Relations, [3]) for declarative model transformations.

Modelware is the technical space [4] of MDE, i.e. a working context with a set of associated concepts, body of knowledge, tools, required skills, and possibilities. In contrast, Grammarware is the technical space of grammars and grammar-aware theories and software. Bridging of technical spaces is specially useful for adopting the benefits of the other technical space [5], e.g. the translation of

© Springer International Publishing Switzerland 2015
A. Pardo and S.D. Swierstra (Eds.): SBLP 2015, LNCS 9325, pp. 112–127, 2015.
DOI: 10.1007/978-3-319-24012-1_9

MDE elements (models, metamodels and transformations) into Grammarware elements should allow their integration into existing tools such as diff/merge, as well as the definition of declarative semantics associated to grammar productions. There are reasonable similarities between grammars and metamodels [5]. Since metamodels are language definitions, there is a relation between them and the concept of a grammar, as well as models conforming to a metamodel are like strings recognized by a grammar. Moreover, syntactical and semantical properties that must hold in a given model to be considered conformant to a metamodel, can be considered part of the semantics of a grammar. We also claim that model transformations can be considered part of this semantics.

In this paper we address the bridging of Modelware and Grammarware by representing MDE elements using Attribute Grammars (AGs, [6]). An AG is composed by an underlying context-free grammar, describing the structure of an Abstract Syntax Tree (AST), together with a set of attributes defined for each non-terminal which allows to compute and pass information downwards and upwards within the AST. In particular, we describe how metamodels can be represented as grammars, and their semantics, as well as QVT-like model transformations, as attributes of the grammar. AGs constitutes an executable method of specification, since it describes only a computation in terms of an AG and then automatically produces a program [7]. In this way we can derive a program for checking conformance and executing a model transformation. We also discuss the practical implications of this approach through the development of a case study[1] using the Utrecht University Attribute Grammar Compiler (uuagc [2], [8]); a preprocessor that generates Haskell code out of AG specifications.

The remainder of the paper is structured as follows. In Sect. 2 we introduce the main concepts of MDE based on a running example. Then, in Sect. 3 we present how models and metamodels can be represented using AGs, such that is possible to verify conformance of a model with respect to its metamodel. In Sect. 4 we present the specification of QVT-like model transformation using AGs. Finally, in Sect. 5 we present related work and in Sect. 6 we present some conclusions and an outline of further work.

2   Model-Driven Engineering

Every model *conforms* to a metamodel, which typically defines syntax and (static) semantics of modeling languages like UML. The MetaObject Facility (MOF, [2]) is a standard language for metamodeling. In few words, a metamodel defines classes which can belong to a hierarchical structure. Any class has properties which can be attributes (named elements with an associated type which can be a primitive type or another class) and associations (relations between classes in which each class plays a role within the relation). Every property has a multiplicity which constrains the number of elements that can be related through the property.

---

[1]   Complete source code of our running example is available at https://www.fing.edu. uy/inco/grupos/coal/field.php/Research/ANII14.

[2]   https://hackage.haskell.org/package/uuagc.

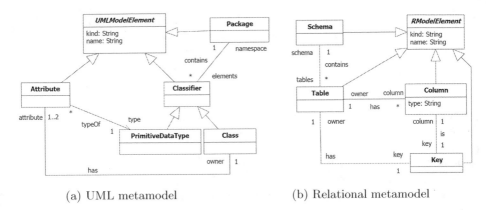

(a) UML metamodel   (b) Relational metamodel

Fig. 1. Exampling metamodels

If there are conditions that cannot be captured by the structural rules of this language, the Object Constraint Language (OCL, [9]) is used to specify them. These considerations allow defining the conformance relation in terms of *structural* and *semantical* conformance. Structural conformance with respect to a MOF metamodel means that in a given model: every object and link is well-typed and the model also respects the multiplicity constraints. Semantical conformance means that a given model respects the invariants specified with the supplementary constraint language.

As an example, the metamodel in Fig. 1a defines UML class diagrams, where classifiers (classes and primitive types as string, boolean, integer, etc.) are contained in packages (association `contains`). Classes can contain attributes (association `has`) and may be declared as persistent (`kind = 'Persistent'`), whilst attributes have a type that is a primitive type (association `typeOf`). Notice that a class must contain only one or two attributes (multiplicity `1..2`), and also that the Classifier class is not abstract. We decided to handle these aspects differently from UML class diagrams in order to have a more complete example. The Relational diagrams metamodel in Fig. 1b defines schemas which contain a number of tables and each table has a number of columns. Each column has a name and a kind, and can be the primary key of the corresponding table.

A model transformation takes as input a model conforming to certain metamodel and produces as output another model conforming to another metamodel (possibly the same). Query/View/Transformation Relations (QVT-Relations, [3]) is a relational language which defines transformation rules as mathematical relations between source and target elements. A transformation is a set of interconnected relations: top-level relations that must hold in any transformation execution, and non-top-level relations that are required to hold only when they are referred from another relation. Every relation defines a set of variables, and source and target patterns which are used to find matching sub-graphs of elements in a model. Relations can also contain a `when` clause which specifies the conditions under which the relationship needs to hold, and a `where` clause which specifies the condition that must be satisfied by all model elements participating

```
transformation uml2rdbms  ( uml : UML , rdbms : RDBMS ) {
  key RDBMS::Schema {name};
  key RDBMS::Table  {name, schema};
  key RDBMS::Column {name, owner};
  key RDBMS::Key    {name, column};
  top relation PackageToSchema {
    pn : String;
    checkonly domain uml p:UML::Package { name = pn };
    enforce domain rdbms s:RDBMS::Schema { name = pn };
  }
  top relation ClassToTable {
    cn, prefix : String;
    checkonly domain uml c:UML::Class {
      namespace = p:UML::Package {}, kind = 'Persistent', name = cn
    };
    enforce domain rdbms t:RDBMS::Table {
      schema = s:RDBMS::Schema {}, name = cn,
      column = cl:RDBMS::Column { name = 'TID', typeT = 'NUMBER' },
      keyK = k:RDBMS::Key { name = 'PK', column = cl }
    };
    when { PackageToSchema(p, s); }
    where { AttributeToColumn(c, t) }
  }
  relation AttributeToColumn { ... }
}
```

Fig. 2. Class to relational transformation (excerpt)

in the relation. The **when** and **where** clauses, as well as the patterns may contain arbitrary boolean OCL expressions and can invoke other relations.

Consider the example of Fig. 2 which is a simplified version of the well-known Class to Relational transformation [3]. The transformation basically describes how persistent classes within a package are transformed into tables within a schema. The relation `PackageToSchema` states that any UML package is mapped into a relational schema. Moreover, the relation `ClassToTable` states that classes marked as persistent are mapped into tables with the same name, a primary key and an identifying column, such that the package to which the class belongs is in the relation with the schema to which the table belongs. The relation `AttributeToColumn` is called from the where clause of `ClassToTable` and maps primitive attributes of the persistent class to columns of the corresponding table. There are also keys, e.g. stating that the transformation must ensure that there cannot be two `Tables` with the same `name` within the same `Schema`.

3   AG-based Structural and Semantical Conformance

As discussed in [5], describing a mapping from metamodels to grammars is in many ways more demanding than the opposite, since metamodels inherently contain more information than grammars, as for example the notion of inheritance between metamodel elements and properties. Moreover, any metamodel can be considered a graph of elements whereas grammars forms a tree. In what follows we introduce how metamodels can be mapped into AGs in such a way that a model conforming with a metamodel is represented as a string recognized by the corresponding AG. We also describe how AGs allow us to address structural and semantical conformance checking as in the MDE world. Throughout this section we also introduce the main concepts of AGs related to our proposal.

Since we are focusing on model transformations, we do not consider some MOF constructs. In particular, we do not consider aggregation, uniqueness and ordering properties within a property end, operations on classes, and packages. Aggregation and operations are not used within transformations, whereas packages are just used for organizing metamodel elements (they can be considered syntactic sugar). Although uniqueness and ordering properties are neither commonly used, they can be considered within semantical conformance checking.

MOF elements can be translated to AGs as follows.

Classes and Hierarchies. Each class is translated to a non-terminal with a production rule resulting from the translation of their properties. If the class does not have a superclass, then its production rule includes a terminal *oid* of type *Int* representing an unique identifier of any instance of such class. Moreover, if the class has subclasses, the production rule defines a non-terminal *child* of type *ClassCh*, with *Class* the name of the class. This non-terminal defines one production rule for each subclass, such that each one defines only one non-terminal of the type of the corresponding subclass. If the class is not abstract, then the child is wrapped with a *Maybe*.

In Fig. 3 we show the grammar resulting from the translation of the UML class diagrams metamodel of Fig. 1a. In uuagc grammars are defined in **data** declarations, which are very similar to Haskell **data** declarations with named fields. Thus, for example, the declarations of *Classifier*, *MaybeClassifierCh* and *ClassifierCh* result from the translation of the class Classifer.

Datatypes and Enumerations. Our AGs are Haskell-based specifications. Thus, primitive types as string, boolean and integer are mapped to their corresponding Haskell types[3]. In the case of user defined datatypes, we translate them in the same way we do with classes. An enumeration is translated to a non-terminal with a choice of terminals corresponding to their values.

Properties and Multiplicities. Properties are defined by a name, an associated type which can be a primitive type or another class and a multiplicity constraining the number of elements that can be related through the property. Within the context of the production rule corresponding to the class who owns a property, we translate a property typed with a primitive type as a terminal of the translated type. Moreover, if the property is typed with a non-primitive type, we translate the property as a terminal of type *Int*, representing the identifier of the element that must be related through the property. If the multiplicity of the property accepts many elements, the type of the terminal is a list of the corresponding type. Finally, we use maybe if the multiplicity is 0..1. More narrow

---

[3] In uuagc everything that is in between brackets is considered as Haskell code.

```
data UML | UML model :: ListUMLModelElement
type ListUMLModelElement = [UMLModelElement]
data UMLModelElement     | UMLModelElement oid    :: {Int}
                                          kind   :: {String}
                                          name   :: {String}
                                          child  :: UMLModelElementCh
data UMLModelElementCh | UMLMECAtt      att   :: Attribute
                       | UMLMECPck      pck   :: Package
                       | UMLMECCla      cla   :: Classifier
data Package  | Package elements :: {[Int]}     -- Classifiers
data Attribute | Attribute typ       :: {Int}     -- PrimitiveDatatype
                          owner   :: {Int}     -- Class
data Classifier   | Classifier namespace :: {Int}   -- Package
                            child       :: MaybeClassifierCh
type MaybeClassifierCh = maybe ClassifierCh
data ClassifierCh | ClassifierChPri pri  :: PrimDataType
                  | ClassifierChCla cla  :: Class
data PrimDataType | PrimDataType
data Class         | Class atts :: {[Int]}       -- Attribute
```

Fig. 3. Grammar for UML class diagrams metamodel

multiplicities are defined as attributes since they are considered as part of the structural conformance checking.

Metamodel. At the top of the grammar we need a root element with a production rule generating every other metamodel element on top of a hierarchy (isolated classes and datatypes are considered hierarchies of one element). Then, metamodels are represented as a list of such root elements. In our example, the root model element is *UMLModelElement*.

The uuagc preprocessor generates Haskell data types out of the grammar declarations. The following Haskell value, with type *UML*, is an example of a model that conforms to the metamodel represented by the grammar of Fig. 3.

```
umlModel = UML [UMLModelElement 1 "" "Package" (UMLMECPck (Package [2,3,4]))
                UMLModelElement 2 "Persistent" "ID"
                   (UMLMECCla (Classifier 1 (Just (ClassifierChCla (Class [4])))))
                UMLModelElement 3 ""          "String"
                   (UMLMECCla (Classifier 1 (Just (ClassifierChPri PrimDataType))))
                UMLModelElement 4 "" "value"   (UMLMECAtt (Attribute 3 2))]
```

Referential and Inherited Properties. Properties are defined in their owning classes, and within a hierarchy they must be inherited by subclasses.

118   D. Calegari and M. Viera

---

set *EveryUMLModelElement* = *UMLModelElementCh Package Attribute Classifier*
                          MaybeClassifierCh ClassifierCh Class PrimDataType

attr *EveryUMLModelElement* **inh** *oid*   :: { *Int* }
                          inh *kind* :: { *Sting* }
                          inh *name* :: { *Sting* }

sem *UMLModelElement* | *UMLModelElement child.oid*   = @*oid*
                                      child.kind = @*kind*
                                      child.name = @*name*

Fig. 4. Attributes defining *UMLModelElement* properties

In AGs, *inherited* attributes are used to pass information downward a tree. We define inherited attributes such that, for a given property, these attributes are copied to every subclass of the property owner. In our example we have that *UMLModelElement* defines three properties (*oid*, *kind* and *name*), thus we define inherited attributes, whose semantics is given by the original terminals of its production rule, and which are copied to their *child* elements. This is depicted in Fig. 4, where three inherited attributes (**inh**) are defined for every descendant of *UMLModelElement*. Semantic rules, starting with the keywork **sem**, define how the value of an attribute is computed. In the case of inherited attributes, is the parent who computes the values for its children. In the example, we define that the values of the attributes *oid*, *kind* and *name* of the child *child* of *UMLModelElement* are the values of the fields *oid*, *kind* and *name*, respectively. Semantic rules have to be defined for every production of all the non-terminal which has the attribute. However, if a rule for an inherited attribute is missing, the uuagc system derives a *copy-rule*, which just copies the value of the parent to its children. Thus, the declarations of Fig. 4 express that, for example, the value of the field *oid* is copied unchanged in the attribute *oid* to all the descendants of *UMLModelElement*.

Some properties are references to other non-primitive elements. In this case, we define a pair of *lookup* attributes for accessing these elements:

attr *ListUMLModelElement UMLModelElement*
          syn *elemLookup$_s$* :: { *Int* → *Maybe UMLModelElement* }
attr *EveryInter* **inh** *elemLookup$_i$* :: { *Int* → *Maybe UMLModelElement* }

elemLookup$_s$ is a *synthesized* attribute; i.e. an attribute that collects information in a bottom-up way. In this case, we construct a function which allows to lookup to an element into the list of model elements using its identifier. Then this function is distributed through the model (*EveryInter* means all the non-terminals but *UML*) using the inherited attribute *elemLookup$_i$*.

For each class with a production rule defining a non-terminal as a reference to other element, we define a higher-order attribute [10], i.e. a local attribute that acts as if it is an additional child of the production (also with attributes).

sem *Attribute* | *Attribute* **inst**.*typ*_   :: *UMLModelElement*
                            inst.*typ*_   = *fromJust* (@**lhs**.*elemLookup*$_i$ @*typ*)
                            inst.*owner*_ :: *UMLModelElement*
                            inst.*owner*_ = *fromJust* (@**lhs**.*elemLookup*$_i$ @*owner*)

Fig. 5. References (excerpt)

```
{
data Type = TPackage | TAttribute | TClassifier | TPrimitiveDataType | TClass
}
```

attr *EveryInter* **syn** *types* **use** { + } { [ ] } :: { [*Type*] }

sem *Package*	| *Package*	**lhs**.*types* = [*TPackage*]
sem *Attribute*	| *Attribute*	**lhs**.*types* = [*TAttribute*]
sem *Classifier*	| *Classifier*	**lhs**.*types* = *TClassifier* : @*child*.*types*
sem *PrimDataType*	| *PrimDataType*	**lhs**.*types* = [*TPrimitiveDataType*]
sem *Class*	| *Class*	**lhs**.*types* = [*TClass*]

Fig. 6. Collecting the types of an element

In the example depicted in Fig. 5 we represent the referential properties for the *Attribute* class. The keyword **inst** specifies that we are defining a higher-order attribute, while with **lhs** we refer to attributes coming from the left hand side (i.e. the parent). Except for the symbols starting with @, that refer to attribute values, the expressions on the right hand side of the = –signs of the semantic rules are plain Haskell code. Since *Attribute* defines *typ* and *owner* as referential properties (to a *PrimitiveDatatype* and a *Class*, respectively), we define higher-order attributes *typ*_ and *owner*_, such that their values are defined by looking up the corresponding elements in the list of top elements; i.e. we dinamically copy the corresponding branches of the three as new children. We ensure that these elements exist by addressing structural conformance as explained next. Notice that we are generating an infinite structure, due to the cyclic references of the model. We make use of Haskell's lazy evaluation to avoid infinite computations, and unfold the structure only as much as needed.

Structural and Semantical Conformance. AGs also allows us to address structural and semantical conformance. Structural conformance requires that the model is well-typed and that also respects the multiplicity constraints. Additional checks are mandatory in the case of referential properties and narrow multiplicity constraints. In the case of semantical conformance, we need to specify supplementary constraints. Besides we do not have a direct translation from OCL to AGs,

attr *Every* **syn** *errs* **use** { ++ } { [ ] } :: { [*String*] }

sem *Attribute*
   | *Attribute* **lhs**.*errs*   = **case** @**loc**.*owner_* **of**
                                 Nothing → ["Type oid" ++ *show* @*owner* ++ "not found."
                                 Just _   → **if** *elem TClass* @*owner_.types*
                                        then [ ]
                                        else ["Type Error for oid" ++ *show* @*owner*

sem *Class*
   | *Class*   **lhs**.*errs*   = @**loc**.*errMul* ++ @**loc**.*errDup*
               -- multiplicity constraint
          loc.*errMul* = **let** *atts* = *length* $ *atts*
                        in   **if** $(1 > atts) \vee (atts > 2)$
                              then [@**lhs**.*name* ++ ": Multiplicity Error: "
                                      ++ *show atts* ++ " attributes."]
                              else [ ]
              -- semantical conformance checking
          loc.*errDup* = **let** *dup* = [*l* | *l* ← *group* (*sort* @*atts_.names*), *length l* > 1]
                        in   **if** *length dup* > 0
                              then [*show* @**lhs**.*oid*
                                     ++ ": Duplicated Names: " ++ *show dup*]
                              else [ ]

Fig. 7. Structural and semantical conformance checking (excerpt)

devised as future work, the potential of AGs allows this kind of checking. Note that higher order AGs are Turing complete [10]. To address typing requirements we define a synthesized attribute *types* (Fig. 6) for collecting the types of an element (its own type and their inherited types within a hierarchy). For synthesized attributes we can define *use* rules for the cases where the semantic rules are not explicitly declared. For example, for *types* the information is collected by appending (++) the lists coming from the children. We also define a synthesized attribute *errs* for collecting errors when checking conformance. This attribute is defined for each non-terminal with respect to their own conformance needs. In Fig. 7 we show some examples of conformance checks. We can see the definition of the inherited attributes and some structural and semantical conformance chekings. In particular, within *Attribute* we check that its referential property *owner* exists and it is well-typed (must be of type *TClass*). Moreover, in the context of a *Class* we define that a class must have only 1 or 2 attributes (multiplicity constraint) and also that the name of an attribute must be unique within a class (semantical conformance). For this last check we use the higher-order attribute *atts_*, giving the list of *Attribute* of a class, we collect their names and check if there are duplicates in the resulting list.

4   AG-based Model Transformations

In this section we describe how model transformations specified using QVT-Relations can be mapped to AGs. As a running example we use the (fragment of) `uml2rdbms` transformation, defined in Fig. 2 of Sect. 2.

The AG specification of a transformation generates a Haskell function that takes as input a model that conforms to the source metamodel and returns a function from an initial model to a final model conforming to the target metamodel. The transformation of the example is expressed as follows[4]:

$$uml2rdbms :: UML \rightarrow RDBMS \rightarrow RDBMS$$

Transformations are performed with check-enforce semantics; that is, first we check if the initial target model complies with the relations specified by the transformation, and then, only in the cases of relations that does not hold, the model is incrementally updated. When executing the *uml2rdbms* transformation to the *umlModel* defined in Sect. 3 with an empty initial target model we get:

```
uml2rdbms umlModel (RDBMS [])
> RDBMS [RModelElement 5 "" "Package" (RMECSch (Schema [1]))
         RModelElement 1 "" "ID"      (RMECTab (Table 5 [4, 2] 3))
         RModelElement 2 "" "TID"     (RMECCol (Column "NUMBER" 1))
         RModelElement 3 "" "PK"      (RMECKey (Key [2] 1))
         RModelElement 4 "" "value"   (RMECCol (Column "VARCHAR" 1))]
```

But, if for example, we use this resulting model as the initial one, then the same model is obtained. In case of models not completely complying with the transformation specification, only the needed elements are inserted, e.g. if only the last column (4) is missing, then the result is the initial model with this column added (and the table updated to refer to this column).

Since the semantic function generated by the AG system should be a function that takes as input a *RDBMS* and results in a *RDBMS*, we define at the root of the grammar an inherited attribute *input* and a synthesized attribute *output*, both with type *RDBMS*.

$$\textbf{attr } UML \textbf{ inh } input \ :: \{ RDBMS \}$$
$$\textbf{syn } output :: \{ RDBMS \}$$

We define a rule as a function that, given a list of relational model elements returns an updated list of relational model elements. Top rules produced by the elements of the source UML grammar are collected (i.e. composed) bottom-up by a synthesized attribute *top*.

$$\textbf{attr } EveryInter \textbf{ syn } top \textbf{ use } \{(.)\} \{id\} :: \{[T.RModelElement] \rightarrow [T.RModelElement]\}$$

Thus, a transformation is defined as the application of the top rules to the input list of elements.

---

[4] *RDBMS* is the data type that represents the grammar corresponding to the metamodel of Fig. 1b.

```
{
type Relation = [ T.RModelElement] → ([ Int], [ T.RModelElement])
}
```

attr *Package UMLModelElementCh UMLModelElement* **syn** *p2S* :: { *Relation* }

sem *Package*

| *Package* (**lhs**.*counter*, **loc**.*s*) = *nextUnique* @**lhs**.*counter*

        loc.*p2S* = **case** @**lhs**.*name* **of**

                pn → *addSchema* (*mkSchema* @**loc**.*s* "" *pn* [])

        lhs.*top* = *snd* . @**loc**.*p2S*

```
{
mkSchema s k pn tl = (RModelElement s k pn (RMECSch (Schema tl)))
addSchema ns []              = ([ oid ns], [ ns])
addSchema ns (r : rs) | ns ≡ r   = ([ oid r],  r : rs)
                      | otherwise = let (s, rs') = addSchema ns rs in (s, r : rs')
}
```

Fig. 8. Implementation of the relation `PackageToSchema` (excerpt)

sem *UML* | *UML* **lhs**.*output* = **let** (*RDBMS elems*) = @**lhs**.*input*

               in *RDBMS* (@*model*.*top elems*)

The rules are created from the relations specified in the transformation. For each relation, we define an attribute at the non-terminal representing the main element of the source domain pattern of the rule. For example, in Fig. 8, for the relation `PackageToSchema` we define an attribute *p2S* at *Package*.

A *Relation* takes an initial target model and returns a pair composed by the list of possibly introduced elements and the resulting target model. The patterns in QVT-Relations are traduced to pattern matching. We use a chained attribute *counter* to generate unique identifiers for the new elements. A chained attribute is a pair of attributes (synthesized and inherited) with the same name that are used to walk through the tree keeping a sort of state; in this case a number.

Thus, for a given *Package* with name *pn*, we create an empty *Schema* with name *pn* and identifier a new unique number. The function *addSchema* inserts this new schema only if an equal schema does not already belong to the list. Equality in model elements ($\equiv$) is defined in terms of the keys declared in the transformation. Thus, if two schemas have the same name we consider they as equals, even if they have different identifiers. If the new schema is not inserted, the returned identifier is the one of the existing schema (not a new one).

Since `PackageToSchema` is a top relation, we use *p2S* to define the *top* attribute by forgetting the identifiers of the inserted elements.

In Fig. 9 we show how the relation `PackageToSchema` is mapped to an attribute *c2T*. This rule only applies if the given class is of kind "`Persistent`"; otherwise the initial target model is returned unchanged. First we apply the relations included in the **when** clause, in this case the *p2S* relation the *Class* inherited from the *namespace_* of the *Classifier*. Then, the model is sequentially (possibly) updated with a new table, column and key. The addition of elements that must be referred by other elements in the model, implies the need to update such other elements, adding their references. For example, to (possibly) add a *Table* we first use *addTable'* to possibly add the new table, in a similar way as we described in the case of *Schema*, and then if the table was added we use *updSchema* to update the schema *s*. After (possibly) adding the new elements to the model, we apply the **where** clause relations to the resulting model. In the example of Fig. 9 we apply the non-top **AttributeToColumn** relation (*a2C*), given a table *t* and model *r4*.

Notice that, for clarity reasons, we are assuming that both the **when** and **where** clauses hold. In case any of them is not fulfilled (returning an empty list of added/checked elements), the pair ($[\,]$, r) has to be returned. Moreover, we did not focus on how OCL expressions (in which QVT is strongly based) can be represented. This is part of future work.

```
sem Class
 | Class (loc.c1, loc.t) = nextUnique @lhs.counter
         (loc.c2, loc.c) = nextUnique @loc.c1
         (loc.c3, loc.k) = nextUnique @loc.c2

         loc.c2T = case ( @lhs.namespace, @lhs.kind, @lhs.name) of
                        (p, "Persistent", cn) → λr →
                          let ([s], r1) = @lhs.p2S_i r
                              ([t], r2) = addTable   (mkTable @loc.t "" cn s [] 0) r1
                              ([c], r3) = addColumn (mkColumn @loc.c "" "TID" "NUMBER" t) r2
                              ([k], r4) = addKey    (mkKey @loc.k "" "PK" [c] t) r3
                              (cs, r5)  = @loc.a2C t r4
                          in  (t : c : k : cs, r5)
                        _                      → λr → ([], r)
         lhs.top = snd. @loc.c2T
{
addTable nt rs = let (s, t)    = (schema nt, oid nt)
                     ([t'], rs') = addTable' nt rs
                 in  ([t'], (if t' ≡ t then updSchema s t else id) rs')
addTable' nt                   = ([oid t], [nt])
addTable' nt (r : rs) | nt ≡ r = ([oid r], r : rs)
                      | otherwise = let (t, rs') = addTable' nt rs in (t, r : rs')
updSchema s t []               = []
updSchema s t (r : rs) | s ≡ (oid r) = addTable2Schema t r : rs
                       | otherwise  = r : updSchema s t rs
}
```

Fig. 9. Implementation of the relation **ClassToTable** (excerpt)

5   Related Work

The representation of MDE elements in terms of a shallow embedding of the languages by providing a syntactic translation into Grammarware concepts has been proposed before [5,11–13]. The translations have some minimal differences between them with respect to the representation of hierarchical elements and properties within. In few words, some proposals model hierarchies as a flattening of elements, move properties from the topmost (or bottommost) element of a hierarchy to every bottommost (or topmost, respectively) element in order to have access to those inherited properties, or discard some intermediate elements within a hierarchy since they do not have any property of their own. Besides these translations generate more optimal grammars, they lose traceability with respect to the original metamodel. Thus it could be neither appropriate for the definition of a model transformation (as attributes related to the main element of the source domain) nor for the definition of the reversal translation from the AG to their corresponding metamodel. Moreover, properties are represented as an occurrence of a non terminal of the typing class, or by-name, depending on multiplicities and aggregations. We use a homogeneous representation by using identifiers referencing elements on top of a hierarchy. Higher-order attributes allow accessing every required property.

With respect to conformance, in [14] the authors propose a formal approach for the definition of metamodels (not based on MOF) using a meta-notation extending BNF and the specification of constraints on models in a formal logic language. Moreover, in [11] the authors define general rules to derive a context-free EBNF grammar from a MOF-compliant metamodel. They also use these mapping rules to generate a Java compiler in which parser actions are added to check semantical conformance. In our proposal, structural and semantical conformance is addressed using the same language of AGs. In [15] the authors use reference attribute grammars (RAGs, [16]) for the specification of metamodel semantics. They basically represent metamodels as in the other referred proposals, but they use reference attributes (the main difference between AGs and RAGs) in order to model non-containment properties. They also define several attributes for representing derived properties and operations (not supported by our proposal). RAGs allow to define a graph-like structure, more similar to the concepts behind a metamodel. However, we can get a similar representation by using a combination of IDs and higher-order attributes.

Up to our knowledge, with respect to model transformations there is only one work [7] defining how to represent a model transformation using AGs. The transformation is represented as attributes and the output is a text that corresponds to the target model in accordance with its grammar. However, this work only present general ideas, not using any transformation language as a reference (e.g. QVT as we do) and exemplifying the proposal using an extremely reduced version of a model transformation. Moreover, they do not ensure that the generated string indeed conforms to the target grammar, as we do by generating an instance conforming to the target grammar.

6   Conclusions and Future Work

We have explored the use of AGs for the representation of MDE elements (models, metamodels and model transformations). Any metamodel is represented with an AG, and models conforming to it are represented as strings recognized by the corresponding grammar. We exhaustively use attributes for handling references between metamodel elements, for structural and semantic conformance checking and for representing QVT-like model transformations. We also developed a case study using UUAGC which demonstrates the feasibility of this approach.

The representation of metamodels and models could be easily automated (as a model-to-text transformation) since there is a straightforward representation of the basic elements (as Haskell types) and the generated attributes directly depend on the structure of the metamodel. In this way, structural conformance can be automatically verified. Moreover, it could be possible to include the automated translation into a modeling environment, bridging the gap between model-driven and attribute grammar practitioners.

By focusing on QVT, we are trying to structure the way we define model transformations using AGs. The case study showed that there is some direct relation between QVT constructs and their AG representation. We still need to study if it is possible to automatically generate an AG from a QVT specification. Our AG-based approach can be classified as a direct manipulation approach, which offers little or no support or guidance in implementing transformations. In this sense, we can explore the definition of an embedded domain specification language (DSL) for model transformations. This DSL could be used for expressing model transformations within the Grammarware technical space, without depending on the Modelware technical space.

Within the case study we addressed the inclusion of OCL expressions. However, further exploration is required in order to exhaustively represent OCL within AGs. This will provide a uniform way of expressing constraints on transformation rules, and on metamodels for semantical conformance checkings. Moreover, it will provide a way of addressing some OCL-based approaches for the verification of a model transformation [17].

Besides an AG describes a computation and then a program is automatically generated, we need to specify some aspects which are abstractly handled by the transformation engine when a declarative approach is used, e.g. when elements must be created or updated. Far from being a problem, this could be useful for the representation of other transformation aspects, e.g. rule scheduling (order or rule invocation), multi-directional transformations, tracing, multiple source and target domains in a transformation, etc. Furthermore, since attribute computations are expressed as Haskell expressions, the Haskell type system (and novel type-level programming techniques) can be exploited to provide partial proofs of properties of the models and model transformations. For example, generated grammars can be represented using the structure defined in [18] to represent correct-by-construction mutually dependent structures and manipulate them in a type-safe way. Further work is required in this sense.

Finally, we need to continue developing case studies in order to strengthen our results. Particularly, complex examples could allow the comparison between our proposal and other transformation engines with respect to execution times.

Acknowledgements. This work has been partially funded by the Agencia Nacional de Investigación e Innovación (ANII, Uruguay).

References

1. Kent, S.: Model driven engineering. In: Proceedings of Integrated Formal Methods, pp. 286–298 (2002)
2. OMG: Meta Object Facility (MOF) 2.0 Core Specification. Specification Version 2.0, Object Management Group (2003)
3. OMG: Meta Object Facility (MOF) 2.0 Query/View/Transformation. Final Adopted Specification Version 1.1, Object Management Group (2009)
4. Kurtev, I., Bézivin, J., Aksit, M.: Technological spaces: an initial appraisal. In: CoopIS, DOA 2002 Federated Conferences, Industrial Track (2002)
5. Paige, R.F., Kolovos, D.S., Polack, F.A.C.: A tutorial on metamodelling for grammar researchers. Sci. Comput. Program. **96**, 396–416 (2014)
6. Knuth, D.E.: Semantics of context-free languages. Math. Syst. Theor. **2**(2) , 127–145 (1968). Correction: Math. Syst. Theor. **5**(1), 95–96 (1971)
7. Dehayni, M., Féraud, L.: An approach of model transformation based on attribute grammars. In: Masood, A., Léonard, M., Pigneur, Y., Patel, S. (eds.) OOIS 2003. LNCS, vol. 2817, pp. 412–423. Springer, Heidelberg (2003)
8. Swierstra, S., Alcocer, P.A., Saraiva, J.: Designing and implementing combinator languages. In: Swierstra, S., Oliveira, J., Henriques, P. (eds.) Adv. Funct. Program. Lecture Notes in Computer Science, vol. 1608, pp. 150–206. Springer, Heidelberg (1999)
9. OMG: Object Constraint Language. Formal Specification Version 2.4, Object Management Group (2014)
10. Vogt, H.H., Swierstra, S.D., Kuiper, M.F.: Higher order attribute grammars. SIGPLAN Not. **24**(7), 131–145 (1989)
11. Gargantini, A., Riccobene, E., Scandurra, P.: Deriving a textual notation from a metamodel. In: Proceedings of Workshop on Milestones, Models and Mappings for Model-Driven Architecture. Volume WP06-02, ISSN1574-0846 of CTITSeries. (2006)
12. Alanen, M., Porres, I.: A relation between context-free grammars and meta object facility metamodels. Technical Report 606, Turku Centre for Computer Science (2003)
13. Grammes, R., Gotzhein, R.: Towards the harmonisation of UML and SDL. In: de Frutos-Escrig, D., Núñez, M., (eds.) Proceedings of Formal Techniques for Networked and Distributed Systems 2004, Madrid Spain, 27–30 September 2004, pp. 61–78. Springer (2004)
14. Zhu, H.: An institution theory of formal meta-modelling in graphically extended bnf. Front. Comput. Sci. **6**(1), 40–56 (2012)
15. Bürger, C., Karol, S., Wende, C., Aßmann, U.: Reference attribute grammars for metamodel semantics. In: Malloy, B., Staab, S., van den Brand, M. (eds.) SLE 2010. LNCS, vol. 6563, pp. 22–41. Springer, Heidelberg (2011)

16. Magnusson, E., Hedin, G.: Circular reference attributed grammars - their evaluation and applications. Sci. Comput. Program. **68**(1), 21–37 (2007)
17. Calegari, D., Szasz, N.: Verification of model transformations: a survey of the state-of-the-art. Electr. Notes Theor. Comput. Sci. **292**, 5–25 (2013)
18. Baars, A.I., Swierstra, S.D., Viera, M.: Typed transformations of typed abstract syntax. In: TLDI 2009: Proceedings of the 4th International Workshop on Types in Language Design and Implementation, pp. 15–26. ACM, New York (2009)

Composable Memory Transactions for Java Using a Monadic Intermediate Language

Rafael Bandeira[1], André R. Du Bois[1]([✉]), Maurício Pilla[1],
Juliana Vizzotto[2], and Marcelo Machado[1]

[1] PPGC - Universidade Federal de Pelotas, Pelotas, Brazil
{bandeira,dubois,pilla,mdsmachado}@inf.ufpel.edu.br
[2] PPGI - Universidade Federal de Santa Maria, Santa Maria, Brazil
juvizzotto@inf.ufsm.br

Abstract. Transactional memory is a new programming abstraction
that simplifies concurrent programming. This paper describes the parallel implementation of a Java extension for writing composable memory
transactions in Java. Transactions are composable i.e., they can be combined to generate new transactions, and are first-class values, i.e., transactions can be passed as arguments to methods and can be returned as
the result of a method call. We describe how composable memory transactions can be implemented in Java as a state passing monad, in which
transactional blocks are compiled into an intermediate monadic language. We show that this intermediated language can support different
transactional algorithms, such as TL2 [9] and SWissTM [10]. The implementation described here also provides the high level construct retry,
which allows possibly-blocking transactions to be composed in sequence.
Although our prototype implementation is in Java using *BGGA Closures*, it could be implemented in any language that supports objects
and closures in some way, e.g. C#, C++, and Python.

1 Introduction

The transactional memory programming model is considered a promising approach to facilitate the task of programming multi-core machines, as it does not
have many of the pitfalls of the dominant concurrent programming model using
threads and locks [31]. In this model, sequences of operations that modify memory are grouped into atomic transactions. The runtime system of the language
must guarantee that these transactions will appear to have been executed atomically to the rest of the system.

This paper describes the parallel implementation of a Java extension for writing composable memory transactions in Java. Programmers define composable
actions that are first class values in Java and can be composed using a special
notation. The high level of abstraction provided by this language is obtained
by compiling it into a state passing monad and we provide two different implementations of this intermediate language using the TL2 [9] and SwissTM [10]
software transactional memory algorithms. Although our prototype implementation is in Java and uses CMTJava [6] as the embedded language, the approach

A. Pardo and S.D. Swierstra (Eds.): SBLP 2015, LNCS 9325, pp. 128–142, 2015.
DOI: 10.1007/978-3-319-24012-1_10

presented here could be used to implement an embedded domain specific language for transactions in any language that supports objects and closures, e.g. C#, C++ and Python. The compiler and examples described here can be downloaded from [4].

This paper is organized as follows: Sect. 2 describes CMTJava, the example embedded language for transactions. In the design proposed in this paper, CMT-Java is first compiled into an intermediate language for transactions (Sect. 3). The interesting thing about this monadic language is that it can support different transactional algorithms (Sect. 4). Boilerplate code to access the internal transactional system can be generated automatically as described in (Sect. 4.2). In Sect. 5 preliminary experiments with a parallel Hash table implemented in CMTJava are shown. Although parallel Hash tables are easy to implement using transactional memory, it is very hard to get them right when working with concurrent lock based algorithms [22]. Finally, we present related work in Sect. 6, conclusions and future work in Sect. 7.

2   Composable Memory Transactions for Java

This Section describes CMTJava [6], an embedded domain specific language for *composable memory transactions* [18] in Java. CMTJava provides the abstraction of *transactional objects*. Transactional objects have their fields accessed only by special get and set methods that are automatically generated by the compiler. These methods return *transactional actions* as a result. Transactional actions can only be executed by the `atomic` method. Transactional actions are first class values in Java and they are composable: transactions can be combined to generate new transactions.

2.1   CMTJava and the Bank Account Example

In this Section we describe the implementation of a *thread safe* Bank `Account` object using CMTJava. A bank account could be described in CMTJava as a class with a single filed `Balance`:

```
class Account implements TObject{
 private volatile Double balance;
```

The `Account` class has only one field and Java's `volatile` keyword is used to guarantee that threads will automatically see the most up-to date value in the field. The `TObject` interface works as a *hint* to the compiler, so it will generate automatically the code needed to access this class in transactions. It also generates two methods to access each field of the class. For the `Account` class it will generate the following methods:

```
 STM<Void> setBalance(Double balance);
 STM<Double> getBalance();
```

The `setBalance` and `getBalance` methods are the only way to access the `balance` field. A value of type `STM<A>` represents a *transactional action* that when executed will produce a value of type A. Hence, `getBalance` returns a transactional action that when executed will produce a Double representing the current balance of the account.

An `Account` should also have methods to `deposit`, `withdraw` and `transfer` money between accounts.

The `deposit` method could be implemented as follows:

```
public STM<Void> deposit (Double n)
  {
    return STM{
            Double b < - getBalance();
            setBalance(b + n)
    };
}
```

This method will return a new transaction that reads the current balance of the account, and increments it with a value n. The `STM{ ... }` block works like the do notation in STM Haskell [18]: it is used to compose transactions. The notation `STM{`a_1`;...;` a_n`}` constructs a STM action by glueing together smaller actions a_1;...;a_n in sequence. The variables created inside a transactional action are *single assignment* variables. These variables are used only to carry the intermediate state of the transaction being constructed and do not need to be logged by the runtime system supporting transactions. To emphasize that these variables are different than ordinary Java variables, a different symbol for assignment is used (`<-`).

```
public STM < Void > withdraw(Double n)
  {
    STM < Void > t = STM{
            Double b < - getBalance();
            if (b < n)
              retry()
            else
              setBalance(b-n)
    };
    return t;
  }
```

The `withdraw` method first checks if the account has the amount of money needed for the withdrawal. If the current balance is less than the amount to be withdrawn, the transaction suspends itself by calling `retry`. Otherwise the current balance is changed by calling `setBalance`. The call to `retry` will *block* the transaction, i.e., the transaction will be aborted and restarted from the beginning. The transaction will not be re-executed until at least one of the fields of the `TObjects` that it has accessed is written by another thread. In the case of the `withdraw` method, when it calls `retry` the transaction is suspended until some other transaction modifies the `balance` field of the account.

STM actions can be executed atomically using the `atomic` method. For example, in Fig. 1 we show an implementation of a thread that atomically transfers money between two different accounts.

```
class TTransfer implements Runnable{

  Account c1;
  Account c2;
  Double money;

  TTransfer(Account c1, Account c2, Double money)
  {
    this.c1 = c1;
    this.c2 = c2;
    this.money = money;
  }

  public void run()
  {
    STM<Void> t1 = STM{
      c1.withdraw(money);
      c2.deposit(money)
      };

    atomic(t1);
  }
}
```

Fig. 1. The `TTransfer` class

3   The Monadic Intermediate Language: The STM Monad

3.1   Monads and Closures

Java Closures. To implement CMTJava we used *BGGA Closures*, a Java extension that supports *anonymous functions* and *closures* [1]. We use this implementation of closures instead of the version available in Java 8 for historical reasons in the project. We believe that the methodology described here can be applied on any object oriented language supporting closures (see Sect. 7 for more discussion on this). In BBGA, an anonymous function can be defined using the following syntax:

$$\{formal parameters => statements expression\}$$

where *formal parameters*, *statements* and *expression* are optional. For example, `{ int x => x + 1 }` is a function that takes an integer and returns its value incremented by one. An anonymous function can be invoked using its `invoke` method:

```
String s = { => ''Hello!''}.invoke();
```

An anonymous function can also be assigned to variables:

```
{int => void} func = {int x => System.out.println(x)};
```

The variable `func` has type `{int => void}`, i.e., a *function type* meaning that it can be assigned to a function from `int` to `void`. Function types can also be used as types of arguments in a method declaration.

A *closure* is a function that captures the bindings of free variables in its lexical context:

```
public static void main(String[] args) {
     int x = 1;
     {int=>int} func = {int y => x+y };
     x++;
     System.out.println(func.invoke(1)); // will print 3
  }
```

A closure can use variables of the enclosing scope even if this scope is not active at the time of closure invocation e.g., if a closure is passed as an argument to a method it will still use variables from the enclosing scope where it was created.

Monads. A monad is a way to structure computations in terms of values and sequences of computations using those values [3]. A monad is used to describe computations and how to combine these computations to generate new computations. For this reason monads are frequently used to embed domain specific languages in functional languages for many different purposes, e.g., I/O and concurrency [29], Parsers [25], controlling robots [28], and memory transactions [18]. A monad can be implemented as an abstract data type that represents a container for a computation. These computations can be created and composed using three basic operations: *bind, then* and *return*. The `bind` and `then` functions are used to combine computations in a monad. `bind` executes its first argument and passes the result to its second argument (a function) to produce a new computation. `then` takes two computations as arguments and produces a computation that will execute them one after the other. The `return` function creates a new computation from a simple value.

The next section presents the implementation of these three operations for the STM monad in Java.

3.2   The STM Monad

The STM monad is a *state passing monad* [3] similar to [5,24]. A state passing monad is used for threading a state through computations, where each computation returns an altered copy of this state. In the case of transactions, this state is the meta-data for the transaction, e.g., logs, buffers, etc. The STM class is implemented as follows:

```
public class STM<A> {
    public { Trans => TResult } stm;

    public STM ({ Trans => TResult } stm) {
        this.stm = stm;
    }
}
```

The STM class describes a *transactional action*. Transactional actions are represented as functions that take the state of the current transaction in execution (Trans) and return TResult<A> describing the new state of the transaction after its execution.

The TResult<A> class has three fields, the first field is the (result) (of type <A>) of executing the STM action, the second (newTrans) (of type Trans) is a reference to the modified state of the transaction, and the third is a flag indicating if the transaction is either ACTIVE meaning the transaction can continue, ABORT meaning that a conflict occurred and the transaction must be aborted or RETRY meaning the transaction called the retry() method.

Once the monad type is defined, we need to describe how objects of this type can be composed by implementing the methods bind, then and return. The method bind is used to compose transactional actions:

```
public static <A,B> STM<B> bind ( STM<A> t, {A => STM<B> } f ) {
  return new STM<B> ( {Trans t1 =>
        TResult<A> r1 = t.stm.invoke(t1);
        TResult<B> r;
        if (r1.state == STMRTS.ACTIVE) {
            STM<B> r2 = f.invoke(r1.result);
            r = r2.stm.invoke(r1.newTrans);
        } else {
            r = new TResult(null, r1.newTrans, r1.state);
        }
        r
    } );
}
```

The bind method takes as arguments an STM<A> action t and a function f of type {A => STM<B> } and returns as a result a new STM<B> action. The objective of bind is to combine STM actions generating new actions. The resulting STM action takes a transaction (t1) as an argument and invokes the t action by passing the current state of the transaction to it (t.stm.invoke(t1)). If after the execution of t the transaction is still active then the f function is called generating the resulting STM<B>. Otherwise the execution flow is abandoned as the transaction was aborted, either because a conflict with other thread, or because retry was called.

The then method, the sequencing operator of the monad, is implemented in a very similar way to bind, or it could be implemented in terms of bind [3].

Finally, the `stmReturn` method is used to *insert* any object A into the STM monad:

```
public static <A> STM<A> stmReturn (A a) {
 return new STM<A>({ Trans t => new TResult(a,t,STMRTS.ACTIVE) });
}
```

The `stmReturn` method is like Java's `return` for STM blocks. It takes an object as an argument and creates a simple transaction that returns this object as a result. It can also be used to create new objects inside a transaction. For example the `addToTail` method, from the linked-linked list used to implement the buckets of the hash table from our experiments (see Sect. 5), returns a transaction that inserts a new element at the tail of a linked list:

```
public STM<Void> addToTail(Integer n) {
    return STM{
        Node a < - STMRTS.stmReturn (new Node(null,null));
        tailList.setNext(a);
        tailList.setVal(n);
        this.setTailList(a) };
     }
```

STM blocks are translated into calls to `bind` and `then` using translation rules that are very similar to the translation rules for the do notation described in the Haskell report [30] (See [6] for a complete description of the rules).

For example, the following implementation of a `deposit` method:

```
public STM<Void> deposit (Account a, Double n)
 {
   return STM{
           Double balance < - a.getBalance();
           a.setBalance(balance + n)
         };
 }
```

is translated to

```
public STM<Void> deposit (Account a, Double n)
 {
   return STMRTS.bind(a.getBalance(), { Double balance =>
          a.setBalance(balance + n)});
 }
```

4   Implementation of the RTS for Transactions

All that was discussed on the last section is related to the monadic layer of our system. But how can we make this intermediate language execute transactions on a real parallel machine? In this section we describe the implementation of two different transactional algorithms under this monadic layer.

4.1   Software Transactional Memory Design Space

Transactional memory was first described as a Hardware feature [21]. This paper focuses on *Software Transactional Memory* (STM), in which transactions are mainly implemented in software, with little hardware support, i.e., a compare and swap operation.

In an STM system, memory transactions can execute concurrently and, if finished without conflicts, a transaction may commit. Conflict detection may be *eager*, if a conflict is detected the first time a transaction accesses a value, or *lazy* when it occurs only at commit time. With eager conflict detection, to access a value, a transaction must acquire ownership of the value, hence preventing other transactions to access it, which is also called *pessimistic* concurrency control. With *optimistic* concurrency control, ownership acquisition and validation occurs only when committing. These design options can be combined for different kinds of accesses to data, e.g., eager conflict detection for write operations and lazy for reads. STM systems also differ in the granularity of conflict detection, word based and object based being the most common. Although CMTJava is an object oriented language, conflicts are detected at *word granularity*, meaning that accesses to different fields of the same object will not cause a conflict.

STM systems need a mechanism for version management. With *eager* version management, values are updated directly in memory and a transaction must maintain an *undo log* where it keeps the original values. If a transaction aborts, it uses the undo log to copy the old values back to memory. With *lazy* version management, all writes are buffered in a *redo log*, and reads must consult this log to see earlier writes. If a transaction commits, it copies these values to memory, and if it aborts the redo log can be discarded.

An STM implementation can be *lock* based, or *obstruction free*. An *obstruction free* STM does not use blocking mechanisms for synchronization and guarantees that a transaction will progress even if all other transactions are suspended. Lock based implementations, although offering weaker progress guarantees, are believed to be faster and easier to implement [11].

4.2   Transactional Algorithms Implemented

We can make the STM monad execute different STM algorithms by modifying the `Trans` class, that represents the state of a transaction being executed, and by modifying the code generated by the `get` and `set` methods for `TObjects`. To demonstrate the usefulness of our design, we have implemented two different algorithms for STM, TL2 [9] and SwissTM [10].

The TL2 algorithm is a classic lock based, deferred update transactional algorithm, similar to the one used in the GHC implementation of STM Haskell [17]: all writes are recorded in a redo log. When a transaction finishes, it validates its log to check if it has seen a consistent view of memory, and its changes are committed to memory. The main difference of the TL2 algorithm is that conflicts are detected by using a global clock that is shared by all threads. Every transacted memory location is associated with a write stamp and a lock (they are implemented as a single versioned write-lock as in [9,16]), when opening an object for reading/writing, the transaction checks if the write stamp of memory address is not greater than the transaction read stamp, in that case it means that the object was modified after the transaction started executing, hence the transaction must be aborted. If the memory passes the validation it means that the transaction has seen a consistent view of the memory.

SwissTM is also a lock-based algorithm that uses a global counter to detect conflicts. The difference is that it combines eager write/write conflict detection with lazy write/read and lazy version management. It has been reported to be faster than other classic implementations of STM, e.g., RSTM [27], TL2 [9]. It is also word based and every memory location is protected by two locks: a read lock (r-lock) and a write lock (w-lock). The w-lock is acquired eagerly when a transaction wants to write to a specific location, thus preventing other transactions to write to the same location. Even though a transaction must acquire w-lock in order to write to a memory position, writes are buffered in a redo log. The advantage is that even though data is write locked, other transactions can still read the original value without conflicting. The read locks are acquired only at commit time, to avoid other transactions to read inconsistent states while a transaction is copying its local view of data to memory.

The use of a global clock guarantees *opacity*, i.e., that transactions always observe a consistent view of memory. This is an important feature if STM is to be implemented as a library. For example, the STM algorithm used in the current implementation of STM Haskell that ships with the GHC compiler [17] does not guarantee opacity. In order to avoid infinite loops or crashes due to using an inconsistent value, the scheduler of the GHC runtime system was modified, so that every time it is about to switch to a thread that is executing a transaction, the state of that transaction must be validated.

The `Trans` class for `TL2` and `SwissTM` can be the same and has the following fields:

```
public class Trans {
    public volatile long readStamp;
    public Long transId;
    public WriteSet writeSet;
    public ReadSet readSet;
```

Other transactional algorithms may use a different `Trans` class, e.g., an eager version algorithm does not need a write set. In the implementation described here both the `writeSet` and `readSet` are implemented implemented using a `HashMap`.

Transactions modify the state of the transaction by calling the `get` and `set` methods of `TObjects`. These `get` and `set` methods are boilerplate code and are generated automatically by the CMTJava compiler. For example, for the `Account` class defined in Sect. 2, the following `setBalance` method is generated for the TL2 algorithm:

```
public STM<Void> setBalance (Double b) {

   return new STM<Void>({Trans t =>
          TResult r = null;
          if (balanceFieldInfo.lock.isLocked()) {
            r = new TResult(null, t, STMRTS.ABORTED);
          } else {
            t.writeSet.put(balanceFieldInfo,b);
            r = new TResult(new Void(), t, STMRTS.ACTIVE);
          }
        r
   });
}
```

For each field in a TObject class, the compiler also generates an extra field that contains the data necessary to access this field inside a transaction. In the example, for the balance field we get the balanceFieldInfo object that contains a reference to the field's lock and a closure used to update the field during a commit. The code for the set method checks if the field is locked, in that case the transaction must abort; otherwise, it adds a new value for the field in the transaction write set.

The atomic method takes as an argument a STM object and executes the transaction described in it atomically with respect to other concurrent calls to atomic in other threads. To execute a transactional action, the atomic method generates a new empty transaction state, and then invokes the transaction:

```
Trans t = new Trans();
TResult<A> r = stmObject.stm.invoke(t);
```

After executing the transaction, the TResult object returned must be inspected. If the transaction is still active, it means that it can try to commit. To do that if using the TL2 algorithm, a transaction:

1. Locks the objects in its write-set using time-outs to avoid deadlock
2. Increments the global clock getting its write-stamp
3. Validates the readset: checks if the memory locations in the readset are not locked and that their write-stamp are still less then the transaction's read-stamp
4. Copies its changes into memory, updates the write stamp of each memory location with its own write stamp and releases its locks.

If using the SwissTM algorithm, the transaction must:

1. Lock all *r-locks* of memory locations it *has written to*, i.e., to avoid transactions from *reading* inconsistent values from memory
2. Increment the global clock

3. Validate its read set, i.e., check that the version numbers of the memory location it has read are still less or equal to the value that was in the global commit counter when the transaction started executing
4. Update all memory locations with the content of the redo log, and change their version numbers to the value obtained when the global commit counter was incremented
5. Release all read and write locks

4.3   FieldInfos and the Implementation of retry

As explained before, the TObject interface is just a hint so that the compiler can automatically generate the code needed to access a class inside transactions. For each field in a TObject class, the compiler will generate an extra field, called FieldInfo that contains the data necessary to access this field inside a transaction.

The fieldInfo object contains all the information needed to perform the validation and commit of fields of TOBjects. It has a writeStamp indicating when it was last modified, a function updateField that works like a pointer to the field and is used to update the field with its new value during commit.

When retry is called, a transaction aborts its execution and it will be only restarted once at least one of the fields of the TObjects it has read is modified. Each field of a TObject has in its fieldInfo object a Vector containing the blocked threads that called retry and are waiting to be awaken by an update on that field. Hence, when retry is called the transaction must insert itself in the waiting queues available for each of the fields it has accessed. During commit, before releasing locks, a transaction must awaken all threads that are waiting in the queues of the fields it is updating.

5   Preliminary Performance Measurements

To validate our system we implemented a concurrent hash table using CMTJava. The table is represented by a Java array that contains in each position a bucket. Buckets are linked list of TObjects. The table is protected by a TObject, and when it exceeds a threshold, its size is doubled. Here we compare the CMT-Java hash table using the two transactional algorithms with the HashTable class implemented by Oracle, which uses native Java monitors to synchronize access and avoid race conditions. In all experiments, hash tables were initialized with 11 positions for fairness with the default of the HashTable class. Operations were defined for a random input from 1 to 1000. The mix of operations was 1 % deletes, 9 % inserts, and 90 % of lookups as this is the most common pattern of access to hash tables [22].

The execution environment used an 8-socket 64-cores non-uniform memory access machine (NUMA) comprised of Intel Xeon processors and 128 GB of RAM. Our experimental hypothesis was that the serialization due to the nature of the monitor in the original HashTable implemented by Sun would impar scalability, i.e., increasing the number of concurrent threads would not improve the number of operations. On the other hand, it was expected that using the TL2 and SwissTM algorithms for transactional memories might help to expose more parallelism and, therefore, allow for less contention and better scalability.

Figure 2 shows the rate of operations by milliseconds in the vertical axys for HashTable, HashTL2, and HashSwissTM, when the number of threads is increased from 1 to 16 in the horizontal axis, for a total of 100,000 operations. CMTJava with the SwissTM algorithm is better than the monitor alternative when the number of threads is greater than four, allowing for more parallelism. Here the early write/write conflict detection mechanism seemed to work better.

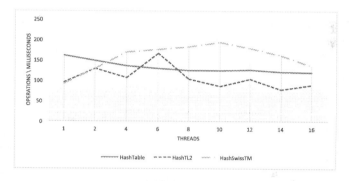

Fig. 2. Rate of operations for different number of threads, 100,000 operations

Figure 3 shows the rate of operations for a total of 1,000,000 operations. Although HashTable is more efficient for a single thread, CMTJava with both TM algorithms is better than the monitor synchronization for a larger number of operations. The SwissTM algorithm shows better performance stability though.

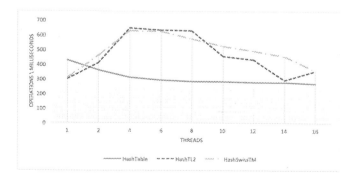

Fig. 3. Rate of operations for different number of threads, 1,000,000 operations

6   Related Work

CMTJava builds on work done in the Haskell language, by bringing the idea of composable memory transactions into an object oriented context. STM Haskell [18], is a concurrency model for Haskell based on STM. Programmers define *transactional variables* (TVars) that can be read and written using two primitives. The readTVar primitive takes a TVar as an argument and returns an STM action that, when executed, returns the current value of the TVar. The writeTVar primitive is used to write a new value into a TVar. In CMTJava, each field of a transactional object works as a TVar and each field has its get/set method that work just like readTVar and writeTVar. STM blocks in CMTJava are just an implementation of the do notation available in Haskell. In previous work [6] we have described CMTJava and also presented a naive implementation of transactions where a global lock had to be held during transaction commit. This simple implementation served only as a prototype implementation to test the language. As the implementation was so simple, it served only as a proof of concept and no performance measurements were given.

Most works on STM in Java provide low level libraries to implement transactions [13,19,20]. Harris and Fraser [16] provide the first language with constructs for transactions. Their Java extension gives an efficient implementation of Hoare's conditional critical regions [23] through transactions, but transactions could not be easily composed. The Atomos language [8] is a Java extension that supports transactions through atomic blocks and also the retry construct to block transactions. Transactions are supported by the Transactional Coherence and Consistency hardware transactional memory model (TCC) [12], and programs are run on a simulator that implements the (TCC) architecture. Deuce [14] is a transactional memory system for Java providing annotations that can give a transactional semantics to a method. It is implemented by rewriting Java byte-codes to add calls to the transactional RTS.

There are many TM libraries and extensions for languages than run on the JVM, e.g., Scala and Clojure. Clojure [15] is a dialect of Lisp that runs on the JVM and has native support for transactions. The functional/object oriented language Scala is a functional object oriented language that supports transactional memory through many libraries, e.g., in [7] a new data type for transactional references is introduced together with functions to read and write these references.

7   Conclusions and Future Work

We have described the implementation of an embedded domain specific language for composable memory transactions in Java. The language is compiled into a monadic intermediated language, and we demonstrated that this monadic language can support different STM algorithms. Preliminary experiments show that, besides the high overhead imposed in implementing monads in a language that is not optimized for it, we could achieved reasonable results in preliminary experiments. Since this project started before the release of Java 8, the current implementation of CMTJava does not use its version of closures. But this is just a low level technicality in the internal implementation of the CMTJava language. We believe that the ideas presented here could be used to implement an embedded language for transactions in any language that provides closures, like Java 8, C++ or C#. An obvious choice would be to implement it in C#, a language that is similar in many aspects to Java. In fact, C# already supports closures through *delegates* and since version 3.0, it has basic support for monads through query comprehensions in LINQ. A monad can be described in C# by implementing two extension methods, `toIdentity` (equivalent to `return`) and `SelectMany` (equivalent to `bind`). If we used the algorithm described in this paper to implement these methods, we could use the LINQ syntax to compose transactions. As future work we would like to investigate new abstractions/constructs for the language, e.g., something similar to `orElse` from STM Haskell or `unreadTVar`[32]. Other lines of work would be to investigate an adaptive STM mechanism for the monadic intermediate language, that depending on the amount of conflicts can change the transactional algorithm used e.g., choose a different contention manager. We would also like to have a library of benchmarks, probably based on the Haskell STM benchmark suite [2]. We are currently working on a operational semantics for CMTJava based on Feather Weight Java [26].

The CMTJava compiler and examples can be downloaded from [4].

References

1. Java Closures. WWW page. http://www.javac.info/, December 2008
2. The Haskell STM Benchmark. WWW page. http://www.bscmsrc.eu/software/haskell-stm-benchmark, October 2010
3. All About Monads. WWW page. https://wiki.haskell.org/All_About_Monads, June 2015
4. CMTJava. WWW page. https://github.com/rafaelleao/CMTJava, May 2015
5. Bieniusa, A., Middelkoop, A., Thiermann, P.: Twilight in haskell: software transactional memory with safe I/O and typed conflict management. In: Preproceedings of IFL 2010, September 2010
6. Du Bois, A.R., Echevarria, M.: A domain specific language for composable memory transactions in java. In: Taha, W.M. (ed.) DSL 2009. LNCS, vol. 5658, pp. 170–186. Springer, Heidelberg (2009)
7. Bronson, N.G., Chafi, H., Olukotun, K.: Ccstm: a library-based stm for scala. In: The First Annual Scala Workshop at Scala Days (2010)
8. Carlstrom, B.D., McDonald, A., Chafi, H., Chung, J., Minh, C.C., Kozyrakis, C., Olukotun, K.: The ATOMOS transactional programming language. ACM SIGPLAN Not. **41**(6), 1–13 (2006)
9. Dice, D., Shalev, O., Shavit, N.N.: Transactional locking II. In: Dolev, S. (ed.) DISC 2006. LNCS, vol. 4167, pp. 194–208. Springer, Heidelberg (2006)
10. Dragojević, A., Guerraoui, R., Kapalka, M.: Stretching transactional memory. In: Proceedings of PLDI 2009, pp. 155–165. ACM, New York, NY, USA (2009)
11. Ennals, R.: Software transactional memory should not be obstruction-free. Technical report IRC-TR-06-052, Intel Research Cambridge Technical report, January 2006

12. McDonald, A., et al.: Characterization of TCC on chip-multiprocessors. In: 14th PACT 2005, pp. 63–74. IEEE Computer Society, Saint Louis, MO, USA, September 2005
13. Marathe, V.J., et al.: Lowering the overhead of nonblocking software transactional memory. Revised, University of Rochester, Computer Science Department, May 2006
14. Felber, P., Korland, G., Shavit, N.: Deuce: noninvasive concurrency with a java stm. In: Electronic Proceedings of MULTIPROG, p. 10 (2010)
15. Halloway, S.: Programming Clojure, 1st edn. Pragmatic Bookshelf, Frisco (2009)
16. Harris, T., Fraser, K.: Language support for lightweight transactions. ACM SIGPLAN Not. **38**(11), 388–402 (2003)
17. Harris, T., Marlow, S., Peyton Jones, S.: Haskell on a shared-memory multiprocessor. In: Haskell Workshop 2005, pp. 49–61, ACM Press, September 2005
18. Harris, T., Marlow, S., Peyton Jones, S., Herlihy, M.: Composable memory transactions. In: PPoPP 2005, ACM Press (2005)
19. Herlihy, M., Luchangco, V., Moir, M.: A flexible framework for implementing software transactional memory. SPNOTICES ACM SIGPLAN Not. **41**, 253–262 (2006)
20. Herlihy, M., Luchangco, V., Moir, M., Scherer III, W.N.: Software transactional memory for dynamic-sized data structures. In: PODC: 22th ACM SIGACT-SIGOPS Symposium on Principles of Distributed Computing (2003)
21. Herlihy, M., Moss, J.E.B.: Transactional memory: architectural support for lock-free data structures. In: Proceedings of the 20th Annual International Symposium on Computer Architecture, pp. 289–300, May 1993
22. Herlihy, M., Shavit, N.: The Art of Multiprocessor Programming. Morgan Kaufmann Publishers Inc., San Francisco (2008)
23. Hoare, C.A.R.: Towards a theory of parallel programming. In: Hoare, C.A.R., Perrott, R.H. (eds.) Operating System Techniques, pp. 61–71. Academic Press, New York (1972)
24. Huch, F., Kupke, F.: A high-level implementation of composable memory transactions in concurrent haskell. In: Butterfield, A., Grelck, C., Huch, F. (eds.) IFL 2005. LNCS, vol. 4015, pp. 124–141. Springer, Heidelberg (2006)
25. Hutton, G., Meijer, E.: Monadic parsing in haskell. J. Funct. Program. **8**(4), 437–444 (1998)
26. Igarashi, A., Pierce, B., Wadler, P.: Featherweight java: a minimal core calculus for java and GJ. TOPLAS **23**(3), 396–459 (2001)
27. Marathe, V.J., Spear, M.F., Heriot, C., Acharya, A., Eisenstat, D., Scherer III, W.N., Scott, M.L.: Lowering the overhead of software transactional memory. Technical report TR 893, Computer Science Department, University of Rochester, Mar 2006 (Condensed version submitted for publication)
28. Peterson, J., Hudak, P., Elliott, C.: Lambda in motion: controlling robots with haskell. In: Gupta, G. (ed.) PADL 1999. LNCS, vol. 1551, pp. 91–105. Springer, Heidelberg (1999)
29. Peyton Jones, S.: Tackling the awkward squad: monadic input/output, concurrency, exceptions, and foreign-language calls in Haskell. In: Engineering Theories of Software Construction, pp. 47–96, IOS Press (2001)
30. Peyton Jones, S.: Haskell 98 language and libraries: the revised report. J. Funct. Program. **13**(1), 1–255 (2003)
31. Peyton Jones, S.: Beautiful Concurrency. O'Reilly, Sebastopol (2007)
32. Sonmez, N., Perfumo, C., Stipic, S., Cristal, A., Unsal, O.S., Valero, M.: Unreadtvar: extending haskell software transactional memory for performance. In: Trends in Functional Programming, vol. 8. Intellect Books, Bristol (2008)

Author Index

Printed in the United States
By Bookmasters